I0117115

REPORT CARD NATION

CHARLES E. SMITH

# Report Card Nation

THE INSIDE STORY

OF EDUCATION REFORM

UNDER GEORGE W. BUSH

*The University of Tennessee Press / Knoxville*

Copyright © 2025 by The University of Tennessee Press / Knoxville.
All Rights Reserved. Manufactured in the United States of America.
First Edition.

Library of Congress Cataloging-in-Publication Data

*Names*: Smith, Charles E. (Writer of Report card nation), author.
*Title*: Report card nation : the inside story of education reform under
    George W. Bush / Charles E. Smith.
*Description*: First edition. | Knoxville : The University of Tennessee Press, [2025] |
    Summary: "In the winter of 2003, a presidential mandate thrust a dozen
    dedicated public servants onto the national stage. Charles Smith, former UT
    chancellor and Tennessee's former Education Commissioner, was one of
    them. The task was to take the Nation's Report Card, a relatively obscure but
    highly respected national assessment, to the forefront of George W. Bush's
    No Child Left Behind initiative, amid a renewed scrutiny of public education
    and a controversial reliance on standardized testing. Smith takes readers
    behind the scenes of the 2003 assessment that would pave the way for public
    school successes and budgetary windfalls but also resulted in inner-city school
    failures and closures, a rise in private school enrollment and the public funding
    of private schools, and, later, the implementation of the ill-fated Common
    Core"—Provided by publisher.
*Identifiers*: LCCN 2024049657 (print) | LCCN 2024049658 (ebook) |
    ISBN 9781621909606 (paperback) | ISBN 9781621909620 (adobe pdf) |
    ISBN 9781621909613 (kindle edition)
*Subjects*: LCSH: United States. No Child Left Behind Act of 2001. |
    Education and state—United States. | Public schools—Government policy—
    United States. | Education—Standards—United States. |
    Smith, Charles E. | Bush, George W. (George Walker), 1946-
*Classification*: LCC LC89 .S615 2025 (print) | LCC LC89 (ebook) |
    DDC 379.7309/0511—dc23/eng/20250225
LC record available at https://lccn.loc.gov/2024049657
LC ebook record available at https://lccn.loc.gov/2024049658

# CONTENTS

# ILLUSTRATIONS

*Following page 62*

President Bush signing the No Child Left Behind Act

Charles Smith testifying at US Senate Education Subcommittee

Charles Smith and Board Chairman Darvin Winick
at the New Mexico governor's residence

Charles Smith presides at a national press conference
as Darvin Winick responds to a media question

Board Chairman Darvin Winick responds to media questions

Charles Smith testifying at US Senate Education Subcommittee

Charles Smith on a Sunday morning special report on C-Span

Historian David McCullough testifies at US Senate Education
Subcommittee

National Assessment of Educational Progress statistics
for fourth and eighth grade reading and math

REPORT CARD NATION

# PROLOGUE

In the winter of 2003, a presidential mandate thrust a dozen dedicated public servants onto the national stage. I was one of them. Our task was to take the Nation's Report Card, a relatively obscure but highly respected national assessment, to the forefront of George W. Bush's No Child Left Behind initiative. We had a steep mountain to climb with much at stake, many obstacles to confront, and little time to accomplish our task. Yet, against all odds, we met our goal, forever changing the way educators, the media, and the general public interpret and use student assessment results.

I was one of two strangers selected by Bush to fill the top two leadership roles. We inherited a talented, highly motivated staff and became a close-knit team by building trust, earning respect, and focusing on effective communication. Together we overcame bureaucratic barriers, avoided political interference, and dodged fallout from 9/11, which allowed us to maintain the national assessment as the gold standard of testing and take the story of the Nation's Report Card nationwide.

A government initiative that works is the exception to the rule. In those rare moments, the how and why of the inside story begs to be told. With true-to-life detail, behind-the-scenes anecdotes, and previously undisclosed official papers, *Report Card Nation* tells one of those stories.

## NOTE TO READERS

This book is based primarily on a combination of my personal remembrances from my time as executive director of National Assessment Governing Board for two terms (six years) and a storehouse of
data from two websites: www.nagb.gov and www.nationsreportcard
.gov. My remembrances are supported by my collection of hundreds
of internal emails and memoranda, reports to the governing board,
texts of my major speeches, entries from my personal diary, calen-
dars, meeting notes, my scrapbook of significant press clippings, and
minutes of governing board meetings and conferences, including
the proceedings of tenth, twentieth, and twenty-fifth anniversary
events.

# 1

ANOTHER MR. SMITH

GOES TO WASHINGTON

In 1939, the year of my birth, Columbia Pictures released a movie entitled *Mr. Smith Goes to Washington*, a political comedy-drama starring Academy Award winner Jimmy Stewart. The movie became an immediate box office hit. Many movie lovers cite it as one of the great movies of all time. Over the years, I have watched the movie at least a half-dozen times, each time fantasizing about someday going to Washington. That was just an idle dream until one day it was my turn to be Mr. Smith on his way to Washington.

As my Delta flight from Pensacola touched down on the runway at Ronald Reagan National Airport late in the evening on January 1, 2003, my heart was racing. I wavered between feelings of excitement, anxiety, anticipation, and intimidation. The next day, I would begin a new chapter in my life, one unimaginable five months earlier. Ready or not, I was on the eve of assuming the role of executive director of the board that sets policy and oversees the development of the Nation's Report Card.

Historically, the Report Card had been essentially a statistical report containing hundreds of pages of assessment results showing what US students know and can do in various subjects, most frequently mathematics, reading, and science. Education researchers had long been the targeted consumers, and the general public had been on the sidelines. George W. Bush changed that circumstance when he signed into law his No Child Left Behind initiative and designated the Nation's Report Card as the program's primary measurement tool. With that action, Bush paved the way for moving the Report Card front and center to Main Street America.

My appointment might not have been so intimidating or exciting in another time. While widely respected by education researchers, the Report Card had languished in the background prior to the George W. Bush administration. However, I knew from my endless hours of prepping that this was not just any time in the history of the Nation's Report Card. Since Bush had made the Report Card a centerpiece in his signature No Child Left Behind program, I knew going in that I would have a front row seat in a major presidential initiative and that the national spotlight would shine on everything my staff and I did.

During the flight to DC, my mind constantly flashed back to all that had happened over the past five whirlwind months. It was hard to believe that only a few months before, in late August, I had been enjoying retirement with my family on a beach near Miami. Four decades of leadership service in multiple roles in my home state of Tennessee were behind us, out of sight and out of mind.

One phone call ultimately changed everything. It came from my old friend Mark Musick, president emeritus of the Southern Regional Education Board. As chairman of the National Assessment Governing Board, Mark asked me to consider becoming the board's executive director.

The call caught me off guard. Another career move was not on my radar screen. "I appreciate you thinking of me," I said, "but as you know, I'm retired."

Mark kindly acknowledged my retirement but noted that he wanted to change that circumstance.

At that point, my political instincts intervened. "Mark, you and I are friends, and I have to be candid. What chance is there that a Republican administration in Washington would embrace a defeated Democratic candidate for governor from Albert Gore's home state of Tennessee?"

Mark seemed ready for the question, responding that it might cause the administration some heartburn. However, he noted that the governing board was independent by law but obviously wanted someone that Secretary of Education Rod Paige could work with. Mark then pointedly said the board was searching for someone who had served as a state school chief officer and who had significant experience in the political arena. "You qualify on both counts," he said.

Despite my resistance, Mark persisted, and within a couple of weeks, I was on a plane to DC to interview with the National Assessment Governing Board.[1]

The private interview took place in a spacious and state-of-the-art meeting room at the elegant Pentagon City Ritz-Carlton just across the Potomac from Washington, DC, and less than a half mile from the sprawling Pentagon. It was an impressive and comfortable setting. After a few minutes of informal meet-and-greet with the two dozen board members, the interview began. It lasted more than two hours.

Although most of the board members were total strangers to me, from the beginning I felt a strong comfort with them. I recognized quickly that this board was different from any other board on which I had served or been a member. Rather than a board of political appointees, these board members were classroom teachers, local and state school officials, parents, state legislators, local and state school board members, and a couple of state governors. Each member held an equal vote.

The interview was structured to encourage conversational interaction. I asked as many questions as the board members did.

---

1. The conversation with Mark Musick occurred on August 12, 2002.

Everyone in the room seemed to clearly see the impact and potential of the No Child Left Behind initiative. Everyone recognized that it was a game changer for the Nation's Report Card. We were all seemingly on the same page. The chemistry was right. I quickly saw that this board got it. The members shared my assessment of the challenges ahead, and they were all committed to rising to the occasion. I left the interview with a sense of excitement, hope, and optimism.

Two weeks later, Mark Musick called while my wife, Shawna Lea, and I were in Chicago for a Labor Day weekend of baseball at Wrigley Field. He quickly informed me that I was the unanimous choice of the board. By that time I had reviewed carefully the thick volume of informational materials the board had shared with me. I had searched the internet for everything I could find about Bush's No Child Left Behind initiative and his education reform efforts as Texas governor. I had learned enough to know that the executive director's role at that moment in time could be a huge opportunity for me to serve my country in a major presidential initiative. Without hesitation, I accepted the position.

In retrospect, that was uncharacteristic of me. Over the years, I had assessed new career opportunities at a slow and deliberate pace, cautiously weighing the pros and cons. Not this time. I was fired up and ready to go. What was different? I honestly don't know. Perhaps it was the sense of freedom that goes with retirement. For the first time, I did not have to consider leaving the comfort of an existing leadership role for the unknown of a new challenge. More likely, though, it was simply a quick recognition that out of the blue I had a second chance to make good on one last dance. I had a chance to wipe away the sting of losing the race for governor in Tennessee earlier in 2002.

For years, I had prepared myself to be governor. During the twenty-five consecutive years leading up to the 2002 race for governor, I held top leadership roles as chancellor of two University of Tennessee campuses, as state commissioner of education, and as chancellor of the Tennessee Board of Regents. No other candidate or potential candidate had those credentials. So, in early 2001, my prospects were reasonably good. I felt prepared. Then a multi-millionaire businessman jumped into the race, and my fundraising dried up. That sealed my fate and choked my dream. Now, however, I had an opportunity to finish my career as a winner.

Aboard my flight to DC on New Year's Day, I sat by the window staring out at the dark sky and reflected on all that had occurred between the call on the beach in August and this plane ride, and I chuckled to myself. Unexpected twists and turns had occurred from the moment I accepted the appointment. My long-planned retirement had been short lived. I'd had to put my beach plans on hold as a move to Washington, DC, took precedence. But the biggest surprise had been the change in leadership at the governing board.

On October 1, 2002, just days after my confirmed appointment, President Bush selected Darv Winick to replace my longtime friend Musick as board chairman. I had never met Winick, which was an obvious cause for concern. However, after some quick research, I found that Winick was a well-respected thought leader and educator in Texas. He had led the effort to staff the US Department of Education when George W. Bush became president and had been instrumental in drafting Bush's No Child Left Behind initiative.

My New Year's flight also provided me time to focus on some mixed emotions. For several years, my family and I had spent the Christmas/New Year holiday at former Tennessee governor Ned McWherter's condominium in Perdido Key, Florida. The 2002–2003 stay with children and grandchildren was bittersweet. Already, the call to Washington had required me to cut short my time in Perdido Key and leave my family behind for the final day or two of our vacation.

But we had recognized from the moment I accepted the appointment that we were moving into uncharted waters, and we all sensed that the move to DC would be a family game changer. I had never worked outside the borders of Tennessee, nor had we lived in any other state. As a close-knit family, we stayed in constant contact. Our two adult children and four grandchildren lived within five miles of our home. Yet I had the full support of my family. They were ready for us to take on the new challenges.

Exiting the plane that night, I formally began a six-year journey unlike any I'd known. I would stand front and center in a major national initiative that had the potential to produce a substantive and lasting change in the way educators, the media, and the general public would interpret and use student assessment results.

As the airport cab transported me the two miles from Reagan National Airport to my new home away from home at Marina Towers condominiums in Alexandria, Virginia, I recognized, with some sadness, that life would never be the same again. At the same time, the adrenaline flowed as I thought about the path ahead—an opportunity to make a difference in a major national initiative. This new opportunity had revived my competitive spirit.[2]

---

2. The content of the first chapter is based on diary notes and later reflections.

# 2

## THE GEORGE W. BUSH

## PROMISE

I slept well, but not long, on my first night in Marina Towers. I woke up about 5 a.m., anxious to step out onto my condo balcony overlooking the Potomac River. With a full cup of coffee in hand, I took a seat and gazed out over the river where George Washington had traveled to his beloved Mount Vernon, the river that divided North and South armies during the Civil War, the river where President John Kennedy often piloted his yacht. Clearly, a sense of history enveloped me as I began my first day as a federal government official.

That morning, I stepped out of Marina Towers full of energy and inspiration to await my cab. During the ride to my new office at 800 North Capitol Street near both Union Station and the Capitol, I focused with great interest on the famous monuments along the way and the reality of my new circumstance became clear.

My new staff greeted me warmly and had homemade treats ready for an informal reception to start the day. I settled into my new corner office, recalling with a smile that Mark Musick had told me that my office would have a view of the Capitol. Technically that was true, but to enjoy that view I would have had to walk out on the ledge of my window on the eighth floor. Needless to say, I never did that.

After the greetings and settling into my office, I spent the rest of the day going through the processes of being fingerprinted, completing security clearances, obtaining a federal identification card and badge, and attending orientation sessions for new employees. I ended the day by shopping for some necessities and then a quiet dinner at Morton's Steakhouse, knowing that the next day my focus would shift to the business for which I had been hired.

My first direct involvement with the National Assessment of Educational Progress (NAEP), commonly known as the Nation's Report Card, had come during my years as Tennessee commissioner of education from 1987 to 1994. During that time, Tennessee was enacting major education reform, and Congress was creating the National Assessment Governing Board to oversee and set policy for the Report Card. The pathways of our state and NAEP intersected as we implemented a new state assessment. The fledgling NAEP governing board was giving states the opportunity to voluntarily participate in a state-level NAEP. Governor McWherter and I stepped up to the challenge, and Tennessee became among the first to volunteer. Thus began a visible and strong movement to make NAEP more of a player in the national education reform effort. The specifics of that movement will be the focus of subsequent chapters of this book.

But the NAEP was not new, even then. The first NAEP assessments had been conducted during the 1969-1970 school year. But the idea for the assessments actually dawned in 1963 during the presidency of John F. Kennedy. The beginning can be traced to a wake-up-call moment for then US Commissioner of Education Francis Keppel. Testifying before a US House of Representatives committee, Keppel fielded a reasonable question: How well are American students achieving? And he couldn't answer it.[1]

The US Office of Education had been established in 1867 to

---

1. *Hearings Before a Subcommittee of the Committee on Appropriations: Departments of Labor and Health, Education, and Welfare Appropriations for 1964*, 88th Cong. 1, pt. 1, at 434–37 (1963).

report on "the condition and progress of education" in the United States. It had plenty of statistics on school enrollment, high school graduates, and class size, yet nearly a hundred years later, it still had no clear data on the central issue in education: How much are students learning?

Keppel became a quick study on how to be responsive to congressional interests. Within weeks following the hearing, the concept of a national assessment began to unfold in his mind. "It has often been pointed out that America lacks standards by which it can measure educational results, and stimulate its students to greater accomplishment," he said in subsequent testimony. "One means to solve this national problem is to work out ways of taking samples of the achievement of students at critical points in their schooling. With this information it becomes possible to plan the needed reform in a precise and pinpointed way. A partial step, therefore, in an overall plan, would be some kind of voluntary examination by which parents and students alike, as well as the schools themselves, could assess their position."

Keppel further testified and "decried the fact that Americans knew more about steel production, garment prices, and the raising of cattle than the proficiency of students in their knowledge of history." He noted the absence of any "present mechanism remotely comparable to the guidelines of the Bureau of Labor Statistics or the Bureau of Standards which would enable us merely to suggest levels of proficiency for our autonomous school districts and colleges."[2]

Over the next few years, Keppel launched Title I of the Elementary and Secondary Education Act—the major federal aid to education program. However, he also took the initiative to establish NAEP as a way to measure student achievement. At first, he had

---

2. James A. Hazlett, NAEP Administrative Director (1969–1974), "A History of the National Assessment of Educational Progress, 1963–1973" (EdD diss., Univ. of Kansas), 352–53.

to confront strong opposition. Critics feared the assessment would improperly expand the federal role in education, so the designers of NAEP focused on addressing those misgivings. Over the years, there have been changes and improvements, of course, but it is basically still designed that way.

The assessment is a survey given to representative samples of students in grades 4, 8, and 12, using essentially the same survey methodology as a poll. This is different from almost all the other tests that students take—the SATs, ACTs, or state exams, which test every student—or every student who wants to take an exam. These tests provide a score for individual students and can have an impact on their grades or their futures. But as a survey, NAEP only samples a representative cross-section of students that it selects. It does not provide results for individual students; only results for the nation, states, and some urban districts, as well as demographic subgroups at each of these levels. The assessment content (known as frameworks) reflects the best and most up-to-date thinking about what should be assessed. A broad base of subject-matter experts from across the nation, along with members of a committee of the board, reviews every test item developed under the specifications resulting from the framework development in order to assure that the assessment content is appropriate for each grade and subject assessed.[3]

If students had to take the entire assessment, it would take them six to eight hours. But using the survey methodology, each student in NAEP takes only a relatively small part of the whole assessment, usually fifty minutes of academic questions. These sections are put together to produce accurate achievement data for large groups of students, but they can't provide sound information on individual students or schools.

NAEP is a secure examination given under scrupulously uniform

---

3. NAEP: A Low-Stakes Test (NCES, May 2012), 4–8. www.nces.ed.gov.

conditions. Trained test administrators employed under a federal contract administer it. However, while NAEP is federally funded, it is distinctively not an inside-the-Beltway product. The making of the assessment involves hundreds of assessment specialists and subject-matter experts from all across the nation who devote literally thousands of hours over a period of several years in the development of the assessment frameworks and achievement levels.

During its first two decades, NAEP tested only national and regional samples of students and produced technically excellent reports, which received acclaim as groundbreaking in the assessment field. But they had little impact because national and regional results were too broad-brush to affect local and state policy decisions. Thus, in the early years, NAEP attracted little notice except from a small number of education researchers.

In the 1980s, reformed-minded Southern governors such as Bill Clinton, Lamar Alexander, and Richard Riley began initiatives to balance investments in education and accountability for results. The US Department of Education began issuing comparisons of student achievement in the states on a wall chart. This approach used scores from the SAT and ACT college entrance exams, the only cross-state data available. But this initiative rightly drew strong criticism, because the data were based on self-selected groups of students going to college, not on a representative cross-section of the class.

The controversy over these flawed comparisons led to the expansion of NAEP. The absence of state comparable data was one of the important factors that led to support for state NAEP. To lay the groundwork, the secretary of education, William Bennett, appointed a blue-ribbon study group. Lamar Alexander, then governor of Tennessee and chairman of the National Governors Association, headed the committee, and H. Thomas James, former president of the Spencer Foundation, served as co-chairman. The committee had twenty-two members broadly representative and conspicuously bipartisan. In April 1988, Democratic senator Edward Kennedy sponsored the main recommendations of the committee's report in a bill, and Republican president Ronald Reagan signed it into law.[4]

This law made three significant changes that have shaped NAEP ever since. First, it authorized NAEP to report state-by-state data. Second, rather than having NAEP remain a part of the US Department of Education, it created the National Assessment Governing Board as an independent governance agency with strong representation from state and local educators across the country. The Alexander-James Report had said that the board should be bipartisan, "broadly representative," and should serve to "buffer [the assessment] from manipulation by any individual, level of government, or special interest within the field of education."[5] So by design, the governing body that sets policy and oversees the development of NAEP was given an outside-the-Beltway character. It has operated that way ever since.

The third change the law made was to give the board responsibility not only to decide on the content of NAEP assessments but also to establish what the law called "appropriate achievement goals" for each subject and grade tested. This became the basis for NAEP's achievement levels—Basic, Proficient, and Advanced—which have transformed the assessment from a norm-referenced to a standards-based exam.[6]

George W. Bush recognized the strength and potential of NAEP. In a speech at a National Urban League Conference shortly before a congressional conference committee sent No Child Left Behind legislation to Bush for signature, the president stressed the need to

---

4. Alexander/James Study Group, *The Nation's Report Card: Improving the Assessment of Student Achievement* (1987).

5. Alexander/James Study Group, p. 8

6. Maris A. Vinovskies, "Overseeing the Nation's Report Card: The Creation and Evolution of the National Assessment Governing Board," (Univ. of Michigan School of Public Policy, 1998), 42.

have "independent evidence that state tests are rigorous and state tests are real." And he added: "Fortunately, we already have a proven way to get the evidence we need, the National Assessment of Educational Progress, or the NAEP. NAEP is not new. Over 40 states now participate. It's not a national test, and we certainly don't need one. But we do need a national report card, and NAEP serves that purpose. We need an objective check on state accountability systems, so we need the NAEP for every state."[7]

Texas, like Tennessee, had volunteered early to participate in the new state NAEP assessment. As governor, Bush made the state NAEP a companion to his own state-education reform initiative. In fact, Texas reading scores in the 1998 NAEP increased five points—two points above the national average. The timing of that good news came in the midst of Bush's presidential campaign. No wonder the Nation's Report Card had his attention as he shaped what would become his No Child Left Behind education initiative. Also, it's not surprising that his program provided the launch platform for the Report Card's rise to prominence.

Prior to going to Washington, I'd had some awareness of the Texas-education improvement initiatives because of my service as a member of the Southern Regional Education Board in the nineties. Many of the initiatives taken by Bush paralleled those of the governor I served in Tennessee, Ned McWherter. I knew that Bush gave high priority to the elementary grades and to improving reading skills. I appreciated his courage to put teeth into reform by requiring reading assessments. I applauded his expectation that every child read at grade level by age nine.

But while aware of Bush's education initiatives as Texas governor, I had paid only casual attention to the early months of his presidency. At that time, my upcoming race for governor of Tennessee

---

7. Remarks of President George W. Bush, National Urban League Conference, August 1, 2001.

dominated my agenda. After supporting and even campaigning for fellow Tennessean Al Gore in the 2000 presidential race, my interest in federal politics took a recess. So when the call came inviting me to become executive director of the National Assessment Governing Board, I knew I had a lot of homework to do.

As I focused my attention, I saw quickly that Bush was a determined young president seeking to replicate for the nation a successful education program known officially as the Texas Assessment of Academic Skills (TAAS)—sometimes affectionately called the "Texas miracle." It stood as Bush's signature accomplishment as Texas governor. As president, he clearly wanted to do the same thing nationwide.

In fact, on his third day in office, Bush signaled his intention to make education improvement the cornerstone of his administration. A year later, with strong bipartisan support in Congress, he signed the No Child Left Behind (NCLB) Act. That legislation required states that receive Title 1 funds to participate in state NAEP in mathematics and reading in grades 4 and 8 every two years. This NCLB requirement advanced dramatically the role of the Nation's Report Card and proved to be a major game changer in the way our nation's schools are measured and assessed. For the first time, the law made state participation in these subjects and grades mandatory.[8]

The No Child Left Behind Act of 2001 required all states to set standards on their own tests using the same terminology as NAEP, which caused some confusion because each of the states had individually developed standards that often differed greatly from NAEP standards. The law also required all states to participate in the state NAEP surveys every two years in reading and mathematics at grades

---

8. Archived: Executive Summary of the No Child Left Behind Act of 2001, United States Department of Education, Last Modified February 10, 2004. https://georgewbush-whitehouse.archives.gov/news/reports/no-child-left -behind.html.

4 and 8—although, in fact, almost every state had already been doing so voluntarily.

Reasonable people may differ, of course, on implementation strategies, but there was a wide and bipartisan consensus among political and educational leaders on policy goals. First, strong support existed for the concept that all students can learn at much higher levels. Second, the prevailing view within the political and educational communities was that the achievement gaps that existed in this country were much too large and were not acceptable.

NAEP had no formal role in the No Child Left Behind law to verify or confirm state test results, and no federal aid money was tied to the test results. Instead, NAEP provided relevant data to inform public policymaking, particularly on two important issues: the overall trends in student achievement over time and the gaps in achievement between different groups in our society. By being the only source of comparable state-by-state achievement comparisons, NAEP had a uniquely relevant role to play in the overall NCLB program.

With the passage of NCLB, Bush seemed to be off and running toward the fulfillment of his promise of major education reform. The new president displayed by word and action the same determination that had led to success in Texas. He quickly assembled a strong and talented team, including a band of talented Texas-education thought leaders who had been the key players in building the Texas-education reform program.

At the same time in Tennessee, two longtime leaders in the final stages of their careers played key roles in uplifting the status and profile of the Report Card in the rollout of NCLB. As the new executive director of the National Assessment Governing Board, I was one of them. The other was Lamar Alexander, former Tennessee governor and a first-term United States senator in 2003. Alexander assumed the role of leading the political fight and providing cover for the implementation of NCLB. As executive director of the governing board, I had the task of serving as point man in revamping the Report Card and taking it to Main Street America.

For Alexander and me, NCLB provided an opportunity to renew an unusual and unlikely relationship that had begun in Tennessee in 1970 at a time when both of us were in our late twenties. At that time, Alexander served as campaign manager for Republican gubernatorial nominee Winfield Dunn, and I had been selected to serve as press secretary for the Democratic nominee, John Jay Hooker. Dunn and Hooker waged a tough battle that ended with Dunn winning by less than a percentage point.

Eight years later Alexander won his own race for governor. Shortly thereafter, in late 1979, he supported my selection as chancellor of the University of Tennessee at Martin. Thus began a friendship that would take several ironic twists over the next three decades. I served as West Tennessee chairman of a coalition in support of Governor Alexander's education reform initiative. When the next governor, Ned Ray McWherter, tapped me to be commissioner of education, Alexander called twice to urge me to accept the appointment. Several months later, both of us were considered for the position of president at the University of Tennessee. Alexander won. As referenced earlier in this chapter, he also became co-chairman of a national blue-ribbon committee appointed by the United States secretary of education to design a governance structure to oversee and set policy for the Nation's Report Card, which developed a blueprint for the creation of the National Assessment Governing Board—yet another ironic twist that paved the way for Tennessee's early entry as a volunteer for the state NAEP during my time as state commissioner of education.

In 2002, at the same time I lost the Democratic primary nomination for governor, Alexander won the Republican primary nomination for the US Senate. Then a few months later, he supported my appointment as executive director of the National Assessment Governing Board.

Assembling the NCLB leadership team early and upfront proved to be crucial, because after Bush's 2001 announcement of his intention to make education improvement the cornerstone of his administration—but before the passage of NCLB in 2002—the Twin Towers fell in New York City. Suddenly, 9/11 changed political agendas at all levels. Bush, the education president-to-be, became instead a crisis management leader and ultimately a wartime president.

At the presidential level, the flag of education leadership that Bush wanted to wave faded to a secondary priority. However, the presence on the ground of the loyal and talented Texas team saved the day. The Texans knew Bush well. They understood what he wanted NCLB to be. With the implied clout of the presidency, they moved the agenda with force and effectiveness.

Too often in a time of crisis, campaign promises and program priorities are sacrificed and lost. To the Bush administration's credit, that didn't happen. Advance planning and execution paid off, and despite the impact of the 9/11 tragedy, the rollout of NCLB didn't miss a beat. That impressed me very much as I began my work at the governing board.

The Bush team also recognized that NAEP had in place a relatively new governance structure—the National Assessment Governing Board—that provided stable oversight and insulation from political intrusion. In one of Darv Winick's first conversations with me, he noted that the Report Card had earned a reputation among educators and political leaders as the "gold standard" in the assessment world and so had instant credibility, something the administration badly needed. He also said that having the governing board in place provided a strong foundation of trust and respect, two crucial elements that I hoped to carry on as, in January 2003, I took my place in the continuing history of NAEP.

# 3

## AN UNCOMMON

## GOVERNING BOARD

No account of the role of the Nation's Report Card in the Bush administration's No Child Left Behind initiative would be complete without an inside look at the enduring success of the National Assessment Governing Board and its unique structure. In more than four decades in leadership roles in my home state of Tennessee, I worked for two higher education governing boards, shared governance in a governor's cabinet with a state board of education and served on more than a dozen governing boards of schools, nonprofits, and business corporations. In none of those experiences did I witness anything comparable to the workings and accomplishments of the National Assessment Governing Board.

The board's strength is anchored by its composition: twenty-six members appointed by the secretary of education after an exhaustive solicitation and review process conducted by a nominations committee of the board. Prescribed by law, the membership consists of two state governors or former governors, each from a different political party; two state legislators, each from a different political party; two chief state school officers; one local school superintendent; one local school board member; three classroom teachers, one from each of the grade levels typically assessed (grades 4, 8, and 12); one member from business or industry; two curriculum specialists;

three testing experts; one member from the non-publicschool sector; two school principals, one from an elementary school, the other from a secondary school; two parents who are not employed by a local, state, or federal education agency; and two representatives of the general public who are not employed by a public education agency. The director of the Institute of Education Sciences serves as a nonvoting, ex officio member.

Governing board staff included the Alexander/James Report in the informational materials provided to me in the fall of 2002 after my appointment. At first reading, I recognized that the report had called for a unique and bold governance structure. However, only after joining the leadership team did I fully grasp the magnitude of the uniqueness and how and why it made a difference. Several factors made it unique.

1. *Membership diversity in geography, race, politics, and backgrounds.* The membership categories included testing experts, governors, state and local school officials, classroom teachers, school board members, business leaders and parents, all seated around the same table with equal votes and the same rank.

2. *Specificity in the nomination and appointment processes.* No stone was left unturned in translating the Alexander/James language into law. It spelled out in detail the calendar to be followed and the mechanisms to be used for seeking, on a national basis, nominees possessing specified qualifications.

3. *Clarity and substance in the governing board's mission and independence.* Alexander/James stressed that "the governance and policy direction of the national assessment should be furnished by a broadly representative board that provides wisdom, stability, and continuity, that is charged with meshing the assessment needs of states and localities with

those of the nation, that is accountable to the public—and to the federal government—for stewardship of this important activity, but that is itself buffered from manipulation by any individual, level of government, or special interest within the field of education."[1]

Over the years, I have seen very few government-appointed committees achieve success in having their recommendations ultimately passed into law. The Alexander/James study group stands as a notable exception. Practically every substantial recommendation became law, and the call for political independence and membership diversity remained front and center in the ultimate legislation.

In the truest sense, the governing board is by design a working board. In a paper commissioned for the twentieth anniversary of the board, former member Diane Ravitch wrote, "Many organizations are staff-run, rather than board-run, or run by a small group on the executive committee. This is not the case with the National Assessment Governing Board." She noted that the board carefully discusses and decides which subjects will be tested, when tests will be given, how tests will be constructed, what kinds of standards will be used to gauge the results, and how the results will be reported to the public. Ravitch added that the board is also responsible for assuring that the assessments are valid, free of bias, and reliable.[2] At the time that the state National Assessment of Educational Progress came into existence, I was the state school chief in Tennessee,

---

1. Alexander/James Study Group (1987), "The Nation's Report Card: Improving the Assessment of Student Achievement"; and the National Assessment of Educational Progress Improvement Act (Public Law 100-297), April 28, 1988.
2. Diane Ravitch, "To Be a Member of the Governing Board: Paper Commissioned for the 20th Anniversary of the National Assessment Governing Board, 1988-2008" (NAGB, 2009), https://eric.ed.gov/?id=ED509384.

which was an early participant. At that time, I had little knowledge about the NAEP frameworks that provide the blueprint for the content and design of the national assessment. If someone had asked me then who was responsible for the test frameworks, I probably would have responded that it was an inside-the-Beltway product. Nothing could be further from the truth. During my two terms (six years) as executive director, I participated in the development of five frameworks. In each case, the governing board's Assessment Development Committee, expertly staffed by assistant director Mary Crovo, sought input from educators at all levels across the country to define what students should know and be able to do in a particular subject.

One of my first, fondest, and nearly most embarrassing moments "inside the Beltway" came with an assessment committee rendezvous my first month in office. Mary Crovo had asked me to address the Assessment Development Committee at its first meeting in a DC Marriott Hotel. I arrived several minutes early, valet-parked my car, and walked into the hotel in search of the meeting room. Not seeing any notice of the meeting, I wandered into the conference area and found a group gathering for a meeting. I entered the room but quickly saw that I was in the presence of a group of morticians. At that moment, I had a sinking feeling. If not here, where? The hotel receptionist told me that my meeting was probably at another Marriott a few blocks away on the same street. With that, I rushed outside and hailed a cab, leaving my car behind for the moment. Fortunately, I made it in time for the start of the meeting.

My speeches of the next several weeks included reference to the "wrong Marriott," the morticians conference, and my first time out in DC. How was I to know there were two Marriotts on the same street just a few blocks apart? The story pleased crowds and gave me an opportunity to poke fun at myself, the "country boy come to town." I even used it in my first report to the governing board in March 2003.

But those early weeks held many lessons for me. I was soon struck by the literally hundreds of educators, curriculum specialists, policymakers, individuals employed in related fields, and interested members of the public who formally participate in the development and vetting of frameworks that determine the content and format of all NAEP assessments, ranging from mathematics and reading to science and history. The process for each framework development spans some eighteen months, culminating with public hearings. The end-product, ultimately approved by the board, becomes the blueprint for the NAEP assessment.

The committees' work in test development does not end after creating their frameworks. After outside contractors develop test questions and submit them to the board, committee members have the laborious task of reading and reviewing each of the proposed items on the assessment in order to evaluate the quality of the passages and the accuracy and coherence of the questions and answers. This is just one example of a true working board.

I approached the whole framework and test development process with fascination: it was unlike anything I had ever seen. Serious-minded educators from all over the United States—only a few from inside the Beltway—bonded in a team effort to produce a quality assessment, consistently fulfilling their mission with enthusiasm and pride in their accomplishments. Crovo was a master in leading these efforts, and she earned the high praise she always received from committee members.

In 2014, the governing board celebrated its twenty-fifth anniversary in DC with a two-day symposium. Speaker after speaker spoke with pride and substance about the board's accomplishments. Under almost any circumstance, a twenty-fifth anniversary is a significant event. In Washington, where the political process and federal bureaucracy often chew up government entities, the board's longevity defied the odds. The board had not only passed the test of survival but had also become a prominent and respected player in the national world of education. Its product had become, arguably, the gold standard in educational assessments, and its impact on educational improvement across the nation had been well documented.[3]

The question at hand was how had the governing board and the Nation's Report Card stood the test of time in such an impressive way. In seeking the answer to that question, I came up with a few key words: respect, trust, wisdom, vision, continuity, tenacity, integrity, commitment, dedication, stability, and loyalty.

The governing board had come into being as the result of the wisdom and vision of Lamar Alexander and the blue-ribbon committee he chaired while serving as Tennessee governor. That committee had recommended the unique structure of the board, the elaborate process for selecting its members, and the effective protections from political interference. In retrospect, the structure reflects sheer genius. It leveled the playing field for all twenty-six board members, providing all selected stakeholders with an equal voice and specific responsibilities. Classroom teachers and parents sat beside governors and state school chiefs with equal power and votes. Not once did I see evidence of a hierarchy or pecking order in the board's deliberations or interactions.

The selection process for members was an innovative gem—one that started with a national call for nominations to fill designated slots being vacated by members whose terms were ending. A board nominations committee, staffed by Crovo, spent hours reviewing nominations and vetting candidates. Ultimately, the board submitted a slate of nominees to the secretary of education. In my two terms, the secretary accepted every nominee without exception. Sophisticated in design and meticulous in practice, the process has

---

3. "Proceedings of the Symposium Celebrating the 25th Anniversary of the National Assessment Governing Board, February 26, 2014," https://www .nagb.gov/news-and-events/calendar/special-events/25thanniversary.html.

produced quality members consistently for more than a quarter century. It left no room for political cronyism and provided no opportunity for patronage. Single-issue members, so common in politically appointed boards, were nonexistent during my two terms.

As for political independence, it would be difficult to overstate the importance of the language that ultimately became the law. Lamar Alexander and his committee wisely anticipated the pressure points that would confront the governing board. The promise of NAEP state assessments under the 1989 law raised the stakes significantly for states. To protect the integrity of the assessment from partisan political influence and to assure the reporting of trustworthy results, the newly created governing board became an integral part of a three-legged governance structure: 1) an independent board comprised of state and local officials and leaders chosen on a bipartisan basis to oversee and set policy for NAEP, 2) a scientifically based statistical agency (National Center for Education Statistics) in charge of administrative oversight of grants and contracts, and 3) grantees/contractors with demonstrated experience to oversee the actual test administration. This structure achieved the proper balance of accountability for producing rigorous results on the one hand and for protecting against federal overreach on the other hand. This ultimate blueprint has stood the test of time, and the safeguards from political interference have actually worked.

In short, the Alexander committee recommendations and the federal legislation that followed provide an excellent model for anyone seeking to establish an independent governing board in a political setting. Wisdom and vision were evident all along the way in the creation of the governing board. Tenacity and commitment were ever-present as Congress shaped the language that put the recommendations of the Alexander committee into law.

From day one to the present day, the governing board has enjoyed strong bipartisan support. The late Senator Ted Kennedy led the way to passage of the law creating the board, and he served as the key protector of its independence until the day he died. One of my great joys of serving as executive director for two terms was working with the staffs of Senators Kennedy and Alexander. They always had our back. Anytime there was even a hint of political interference, they quickly slapped it down. The tenacity and commitment of bipartisan leadership to support and protect the National Assessment Governing Board's independence can't be overstated.

Other key words have defined the governing board's success over the years. Continuity. Stability. Loyalty. Integrity. Dedication. At the time of the twenty-fifth anniversary, the board had been led by only three chairmen and three executive directors. Three key staff members had served from the beginning. From day one, all of us (governing board, staff, Congress, and the US Department of Education) believed that maintaining NAEP as the gold standard in the world of testing and protecting the board's independence were top priorities.

In my remarks at the twenty-fifth anniversary celebration, I commented on why the governing board had not only survived but had also gained stature and respect in the politically charged environment of our nation's capital. "Stated simply," I said, "the governing board's creators got it right. The nation's political leadership consistently provided bipartisan support and protection. The board leadership and members provided continuity, stability, and loyalty. Its staff stayed the course."[4]

That formula has worked for more than a quarter century. It's my great hope that present and future leaders will continue to nurture and support the Nation's Report Card.

---

4. "Proceedings of the Symposium Celebrating the 25th Anniversary of the National Assessment Governing Board, February 26, 2014," https://www.nagb.gov/content/dam/nagb/en/images/25th-anniversary/documents/smith-remarks.pdf.

# 4

## OFF AND RUNNING

Several weeks before taking office as the executive director of the National Assessment Governing Board, I saw early signs that the Bush team was serious-minded, focused, and nonpartisan in their commitment to No Child Left Behind and to their support for the Nation's Report Card. By appointing Darv Winick to the chairmanship of the National Assessment Governing Board, Bush had clearly signaled that the Report Card would be a primary player in the NCLB initiative. In addition, Winick's early actions solidified my belief that our program was in good hands. Even though we had never met prior to my appointment, he wasted little time in extending the symbolic hand of friendship. On his first day as chairman, October 1, 2002—a day after I had learned of his appointment and three months before I was scheduled to take office—Winick called me. At that moment, my son, Chip, and I were in Atlanta attending an Atlanta Braves National League Championship Series playoff game with San Francisco. The game had just begun, and the noise level was deafening. I quickly retreated to the quieter exit ramps leading out of the stadium to accept his gracious congratulations. That phone call sealed the deal and assured me that I had made the right decision.

A month later, Winick repeated and amplified his positive tone by inviting my wife and me to attend the governing board's November meeting in Alexandria as special guests. As we walked into the Alexandria, Virginia, hotel ballroom to attend that meeting, I felt as if

I had entered a meeting of the British Parliament sans the color and pageantry but with all the majesty. In the center of the room stood a huge, oblong table with chairs framing all sides. I quickly sized up the parliament-like seating arrangement, a symbol of the shared governance that shaped the Nation's Report Card. Separate sections of seats surrounded the table where board members were seated. Governing board staff had a section. The NCES, National Center for Education Statistics, had an assigned section, as did the government contractors who built and delivered the national assessment. Then, of course, another section held the media. Shawna Lea and I received prominent seating on the first row of the section reserved for visitors. I had often wondered what it might be like to be on the national stage, and that day I found out.

In the meeting, Winick wasted no time taking charge as the new chairman. Then, surprisingly, he gave me a rousing and enthusiastic introduction, stating among other things what he had told me previously: that if the board had reached out to central casting for an executive director, they could not have found a more qualified candidate.

When the board broke for lunch, the first person who came over to introduce herself was Beth Ann Bryan. I immediately recognized her name as the Bush administration's political operative inside the US Department of Education. I didn't know what to expect, but she relieved my suspense in short order. Bryan told me bluntly that my candidacy had originally caused some "heartburn" in the Bush White House, the same word Mark Musick had used in August when I had questioned whether the Bush White House would consider a Tennessee Democrat for such a high-profile position. Bryan followed her words with a quick smile and told me that they had checked me out thoroughly and that I had obviously passed the test. It was heartwarming to hear directly from her that Republican Senator Lamar Alexander had given me a "big thumbs up" and that Republican Governor Don Sundquist had told her that the White

House could not find anyone more capable of working across political lines, as demonstrated by my years of leadership in Tennessee. In my first week in office, Winick flew from his home in Texas to DC to meet with me. He asked assistant director Ray Fields and me to join him and Bryan for lunch at a popular Pennsylvania Avenue restaurant. During lunch, although talk did turn to the business at hand, we focused much of the conversation simply on getting to know each other. I left the restaurant with a good sense of the energy, commitment, expertise, and comradery of the leadership team I would be working with, and I liked it very much.

Following lunch, Winick took Fields and me to the White House for an introductory meeting with the chief domestic policy aide to the president, Margaret Spellings, who later became Secretary of Education. My transition to DC was moving quickly and substantively.

As executive director, I devoted most of my early weeks to multiple meetings with key officials in both the political and educational arenas in Washington. I also had discussions with state and local educators across the nation. I recognized the need to engage in a fast-track learning process, because the No Child Left Behind train had already left the station as I jumped aboard. I needed to know quickly how much support the Nation's Report Card and the governing board had among the various constituency leadership groups. How much did they know about who we were? Did they understand what our role was in NCLB? What were their ideas about how to fulfill our mandated role in assessments? With the full support and participation of Darv Winick and assistant director Ray Fields, we launched a full court press to meet personally with all key congressional members and their staffs.

In short order, it became abundantly clear to me that officials on Capitol Hill, in the White House and the Department of Education, and within the Washington education establishment knew and cared a great deal about the Nation's Report Card and its governing board. They respected the Report Card, their shorthand name for the National Assessment of Educational Progress or NAEP. They clearly recognized and supported the need for the governing board's independence, valued its credibility, and viewed the national assessments as central to the No Child Left Behind initiative. Most significantly, at a time when partisanship was sharply rising in the political world, the Report Card and our governing board had clear bipartisan support. On the Republican side, Presidents Ronald Reagan, George H. W. Bush, and George W. Bush all strongly and consistently supported the Report Card and the governing board, as did House Education Committee Chairman John Boehner and Senate leader Lamar Alexander. On the other side of the political aisle, no national political leader stood taller in support than Senator Ted Kennedy. President Bill Clinton was an early proponent of the Report Card and creation of the governing board. The list goes on, but to underscore the bipartisanship I can honestly say that in my two terms (six years) as executive director not a single United States senator or House representative at any level ever challenged the validity of the Report Card or the authority of the governing board.

So, inside the Beltway, we started with strong support and trust. The doors of opportunity stood open for us. However, it soon became clear that outside the Beltway, we had a lot of work to do to transport the Report Card from the backrooms of researchers to Main Street America. In general, state and local educators and public officials knew very little about the Report Card and even less about its prescribed role in the No Child Left Behind program. Implementation processes provided limited time for local and state officials to get up to speed. NCLB mandates to build state assessments, establish achievement levels, and report disaggregated results represented huge changes at the state level. In a sense, states suddenly faced the reality of flying a plane that was still being constructed.

My staff and I concluded early that our challenge was a bit different from that of the officials who had the task of building and implementing the No Child Left Behind program. NCLB had to be built from scratch with no track record and lots of unknowns for local and state leaders. While the Report Card had a historically low profile at the state and local levels, at least it had credibility that had been earned over the years. Thanks to the hard work, strong dedication, and keen wisdom of the governing board's early leaders—people such as Roy Truby, Mark Musick, Michael Nettles, Checker Finn, Dan Taylor and others who served during the formative years—the Nation's Report Card, at the time of my arrival, was viewed widely in political, professional, and educational circles as the gold standard of assessments. The Report Card, the NAEP, was and had been the rock of stability in a national and state assessment environment often marked by instability and ever-changing standards. Outside the Beltway, the NAEP had generally been quietly accepted, politely critiqued, and mildly noticed. However, change was in the air: The No Child Left Behind initiative had placed the Nation's Report Card and its governing board on the front row of a national stage.

Fortunately, I had inherited an incredibly talented and committed staff. Three key assistant directors—Mary Crovo, Ray Fields, and Larry Feinberg—had all been on staff from the beginning of the governing board's creation. Crovo was soft-spoken and deeply intelligent. Prior to joining the board staff, she had served as chief of research and evaluation for the Maryland State Department of Education. Fields was a profound thinker, always optimistic. Prior to becoming a board staff member, Fields had served several years as a legislative aide for education in the US House of Representatives. Feinberg was somewhat the extrovert on the team, a great writer but not known for keeping a clean desk. He came to the board staff after several years as a reporter for the *Washington Post*. While the three key staff members had different career experiences, they had one thing in common: They believed that what they were doing was extremely important. Working for the Nation's Report Card was not just a job for them; it was a calling. They were totally committed to nurturing, sustaining, and protecting the integrity of the Report Card. I was only the second executive director they had served, but they received me with open arms. We all saw that No Child Left Behind provided an opportunity to take the Nation's Report Card to unprecedented levels.

Even in those early weeks with my talented staff, I recognized that they knew what they were doing, and they were doing it well. My advice to myself was to stay out of the way and give them lots of flexibility. They were like performers in a symphony—each was an artist with unique talents, proud and protective of the role they played in the national assessment, and untiring and uncompromising in their commitment to their task. As I commented to Winick one day, my primary challenge inside the office was simply to monitor carefully the interaction and inevitable conflicts that occur when extremely talented and highly motivated people disagree from time to time. I always knew, however, that in the end, the staff would pull together and do what was right for the Nation's Report Card.

We all saw that the No Child Left Behind initiative had captured the attention of our nation in an unprecedented manner. From my perspective, its sweeping and broad-based impact on our national education landscape reminded me of the education reform during the administration of President Lyndon Johnson. However, the differences between the two reform efforts were more dramatic than the similarities. While both reforms increased significantly the flow of federal funding into local school systems, No Child Left Behind was, in my judgment, unprecedented in its mandated expectations in return for funding.[1]

My first "official" moment with the full governing board came in March 2003 at a quarterly meeting held in Washington. After

---

1. The descriptions of my staff's early organization and strategic efforts rely on my diary notes and later reflections.

slightly more than two months of fast-paced learning, the time had come for me to prove myself fit and ready to serve the board for whom I worked. The executive director's report had historically been the first item on the board agenda, and I knew my first report would be a tough test of my leadership. While somewhat nervous about the meeting, I felt prepared and confident as I took the podium that day.

Today the spotlight on what we do and how we do it has never been brighter. The stakes have never been higher. The scrutiny has never been greater. The margin for error has never been smaller.

In short, we have our work cut out for us. We must make every effort to sustain NAEP as the gold standard of assessment. We must do everything possible to protect the credibility and independence of the process that produces NAEP results and of the NAEP results themselves.

We must redouble our efforts to put in place policies and guidelines that ensure that our assessments withstand the scrutiny, criticism, and challenges that inevitably will increase manyfold in the years ahead.

Having given thousands of speeches over my four decades of leadership in Tennessee, I had learned how to read an audience. I always scanned the crowd, looking for body language, facial expressions, or any visual sign of interest. On this day, I paid particular attention, and I remember being stimulated by the attentiveness of every member of the board and even the NCES staff, contractors, other attendees.

I continued.

Our nation today has education reform with consequences, and assessment is at the heart of the initiative. I can recall as a former state commissioner of education the scant attention state and local officials generally paid to federal legislation. In large measure, the feds were out of sight and out of mind.

Not so today. In my early days as executive director, I have seen clear evidence firsthand that what's happening in our nation's capital is very much in sight and very much on the mind all across America. It is also shaping state agendas, dominating education conferences, and changing dramatically the way state and local school officials are making decisions. In large measure, this new national reality has positive consequences for those of us in this room. It places greater importance on all that we do. It moves the value of assessments and standards to a higher level of attention. It gives us even more reason to protect, nurture, and sustain all that has made NAEP the nation's gold standard of assessment.

I noted, however, that by mandating state-designed and delivered tests as well as requiring that all states use the fourth- and eighth-grade NAEP assessments in reading and math, No Child Left Behind legislation may have inadvertently discouraged the continued use of other NAEP assessments by the states. I voiced concern that, inevitably, the pressures associated with new mandated assessments would create the temptation at the state level to cut back on non-mandated assessments such as science, history, civics, geography, and writing.

We must be proactive in selling the notion that NAEP is a lot more than its assessments at grades 4 and 8 in reading and math. We must be aggressive in promoting the value of all of our assessments. We must be forceful in advocating that NAEP must continue to serve the whole breadth of American education and not become just a measurement of one part of it. It would be a shame to see all the 'value-added' that the No Child Left Behind initiative has provided NAEP be diminished by a decline in the use of our voluntary assessments.

Our challenge is to choose wisely as we confront the new pressures, conflicting signals, and changing expectations of our constituencies. Stated another way, we must evaluate thoughtfully and objectively all that we do and have done. We must determine what is worthy of preserving, protecting, and nurturing. And, then we must be prepared to explain, justify, and defend what we have in place.

At the same time, we must be equally diligent and courageous in dealing with assessment policies, processes, and products that our review determines to be obsolete, inadequate, or non-productive. Whether the topic is reading frameworks, background questions, history assessment timetables, or NAEP evaluations, judgments must be made. What we must strive for is informed judgments, based on broad-based input, objective data, serious deliberation, and a strong dose of just plain old common sense.

I cautioned that the governing board no longer had any margin of error and that we had to get it right the first time. I stressed that we had to be able to explain what we were doing and why, in language that all segments of the public could understand. "Stated simply," I said, "the whole world is now watching what we are doing."[2]

With those words, I closed my first governing board presentation sixty-four days into my tenure as executive director. I had hoped my message would be on target and resonate with the board members. Thankfully, I didn't have to wait long to find out. Everyone sprang to their feet and gave me a lengthy standing ovation. The staff told me later that had never happened at a board meeting. I was both relieved and gratified. As a team, we were off and running with an ambitious agenda. More than that, we were on the same page.

---

2. Charles E. Smith to National Assessment Governing Board, report, March 2003.

# 5

## TURF WARS

Shortly before my arrival in DC, President Bush signed a law creating the Institute of Education Sciences (IES). Imbedded in that
action was a provision that proved to be a game changer for the
governing board and paved the way for moving the Nation's Report
Card from the backroom to Main Street. The new law, passed on
November 2, 2002, stated that the National Assessment Governing
Board shall "plan and execute the initial public release of National
Assessment of Educational Progress report ... develop guidelines for
reporting and disseminating results ... develop a process for review
of the assessment ... (and) exercise its responsibilities independent
of the Secretary and other offices and officers of the Department."[1]

To an outsider, the language of the new law may be viewed as
so much bureaucratic mumbo jumbo. However, inside the world
of education, this dramatic and consequential action came with a
significant history. Historically, the National Center for Education
Statistics (NCES) within the Department of Education had held

---

1. "Education Sciences Reform Act of 2002," Public Law 107-279, Approved
   November 5, 2002, https://www.govinfo.gov/content/pkg/COMPS-747/pdf
   /COMPS-747.pdf; John H. Stevens, "Getting the Word Out about the
   National Assessment: Paper Commissioned for the 20th Anniversary of the
   National Assessment Governing Board 1988-2008" (NAGB, March 2009),
   18. https://files.eric.ed.gov/fulltext/ED509381.pdf.

primary jurisdiction over all aspects of the Nation's Report Card. When the governing board was created in 1989, several important responsibilities had shifted away from NCES. Under the new law, the board set the schedule of assessments, which in turn drove the budget, determined the test content and approved all assessment items, and set achievement levels for reporting results. Yet, the question of who controlled the release of the national assessment reports remained unresolved and unclear in the governing board's first decade.

Then two incidents—one in 1992, the other in 1998—caused lawmakers to be concerned about what several members of Congress called the politicization of the Nation's Report Card. By law, premature release of assessment results is specifically prohibited and punishable. The same goes for any politicization of the release. But in 1992 President George H. W. Bush made premature comments about assessment results the day before the Report Card's public release. Lawmakers generally viewed this as an unintended transgression. Then in 1998, presidential candidate Al Gore stirred a political outcry by taking a lead role in announcing Report Card results at the release event and falsely claiming credit. The governing board spoke out publicly against both of these incidents at the time of their occurrence.[2]

Gore's unprecedented action was considered the more serious of the two transgressions, and it triggered a movement in Congress that led eventually to the language included in the legislation creating the Institute of Education Sciences, or IES. Passage of the law creating IES was just the beginning of what was to become one of

---

2. Subcommittee on Oversight and Investigations Hearing, U.S. House of Representatives, May 27, 1999, Educational Resources Information Center (ERIC), Document ED440373, p. 7. https://eric.ed.gov/fulltext/ED440373 .pdf.

the most consequential turf battles between the National Center for Education Statistics and the governing board. And it happened in the early days of my watch.

In fact, that issue was the subject of my first internal memo, written on January 5, 2003, to governing board Deputy Director Sharif Shakrani and Assistant Director Ray Fields in preparation for our meeting later that week with the institute's director, Russ Whitehurst. In that memo, I stated that my review of the background information provided by staff "has led me to the conclusion that we have before us a three-dimensional issue with far-reaching potential for impact on the relationship between NCES and NAGB, the implementation of No Child Left Behind, and the independence and credibility of NAGB. The three dimensions are political, legal, and programmatic."

If the board was going to act in concert, I knew I needed to diagnose the situation in some detail. So I went on.

Even to a layman, the language of the new law is clear and non-debatable: NAGB has been given the responsibility for planning and executing the initial public release of NAEP assessment reports. Ray's excellent analysis, particularly the side-by-side comparisons, reflects the reality of the substance and intent of the legislation. However, [Associate Commissioner of NCES] Peggy Carr's correspondence to Russ Whitehurst and his strongly worded concurrence with her position make clear that NCES rejects the language and disagrees with the interpretations.

Peggy and Russ are forceful and specific in their stated disagreements with the NAGB interpretation. What is missing is any sense of what they believe the new law does mandate and/or change. Do we have any knowledge of what they believe needs to be done to comply with the law? Clearly, the law explicitly mandates a change. If it is not what we think it is, then what do Whitehurst and Carr think it is? There is no way anyone could legitimately interpret the law change as a mandate for maintaining the status quo.

I stressed that the National Assessment Governing Board faced a serious political dilemma, noting that if we accepted the positions of Carr and Whitehurst, we would likely run head-on into a conflict with the congressional leaders who had inserted the language into the law. Moreover, we would risk compromising the NAGB's credibility.

"On the other hand, if we stand firm on the position we have taken thus far, we inevitably will be placed in a serious conflict situation with Peggy, Russ, and perhaps others in the Department of Education," I wrote. "Either way, we lose. Where is the middle ground? Where is the compromise opportunity?" For me, this was not a rhetorical question. I continued.

Clearly, the integrity, credibility, and independence of NAGB are at stake. Furthermore, this issue is a test case of what will likely be a frequent challenge for NAGB over the next several months. Now that national assessments have become high stakes for all concerned, NAGB will clearly be in the eye of the storm for at least the next two years as NCLB is implemented. We will be scrutinized and critiqued as never before. How we handle this could very well set the course for the handling of future conflicts.

The bottom line is that we need closure on this issue as soon as possible, and that closure must protect the integrity, credibility, and independence of NAGB and provide a politically viable compromise. This is no small order. Again, legally we are clearly where we should be; politically we are on shaky ground with more potential to lose than to gain; and programmatically does it really make any difference? From the perspective of someone who has spent a lifetime in the trenches of turf battles and political infighting, this one is multi-dimensional and complicated.[3]

At the time, I didn't attach a lot of importance to this memo. Only later did I learn that, from the perspective of my staff and some board members, that memo, written in the first days of my appointment, spoke volumes about my style of leadership: I would be firm, cautious, thorough, fair, and protective of our mission.

The meeting with Whitehurst and Carr, both true professionals, took place at a neutral site in a downtown DC restaurant. The session was reasonably pleasant but failed to change anyone's mind. A scientist by training and analytical by nature, Whitehurst viewed the Report Card as any purist would: The data had to be technically correct no matter how complex the reports had to be. Carr, unlike Whitehurst, was not a political appointee. As a career employee, she had built a solid reputation in the assessment world. In our meeting, she and Whitehurst based their position of opposition on the language of a separate piece of legislation that gave the Center for Education Statistics authority over the release of data in general. It was clear that we were in for a long battle.

Fortunately, the new governing board chairman, Darv Winick, understood the issue at hand and strongly supported our staff position about the law. He and John Stevens, chairman of the board's Reporting and Dissemination Committee, became directly involved in the discussion with officials for the National Center for Education Statistics and the Institute of Education Sciences. Winick and Whitehurst were longtime friends and had mutual respect for one another, a factor that kept discussions civil most of the time.

---

3. Charles E. Smith to Sharif Shakrani and Ray Fields, memorandum, January 5, 2003.

As the discussions continued and intensified, the No Child Left Behind train had long ago left the station. The first results of assessments under NCLB were due for release in 2003. With resolution of the legal issue still unsettled, the National Center for Education Statistics and the National Assessment Governing Board were forced to embrace a transitional mode with shared responsibilities. The governing board assumed some new responsibilities, but in large measure, as the two agencies prepared for release of the 2003 reports, the old way of working continued.

In the meantime, John Stevens and his Reporting and Dissemination Committee moved forward with discussing and drafting new policies that implemented the provisions of the law. As the process stretched from weeks into months, staff and governing board members at times felt frustrated. We knew what had to be done, but bureaucratic turf battles continued to slow down our forward movement. Fortunately, board members and staff never let the pace affect our resolve to achieve the ultimate goals.

By September 2004, the committee members were finalizing their work. In preparation for meeting with them, I sent Chairman Stevens a memo.

> Traditions, mindsets, and ways of doing things in general die slowly and painfully within a bureaucracy. It is predictable that the first line of resistance from NCES will simply be a sweeping challenge to NAGB's right to tell NCES how to present NAEP reports. We will likely be given multiple reasons why format guidelines violate NCES report specifications, why graphic models produced by Ogilvy [an outside contractor we had employed] fail to measure up to research standards, why NAEP data on the web is outside of NAGB's jurisdiction, etc.
>
> I believe our first task in the committee meeting is to plant the flag of authority that NAGB possesses to make the decisions that are on the table. The first page of the introduction

to the policy statement that Larry Feinberg has prepared cites specifically the range of authority and responsibility that NAGB has been given by Congress. In addition, Ray Fields will be prepared to speak in detail about the language of the law if circumstances of the discussion merit elaboration.

My memo stressed the importance of building on an existing foundation, namely on the major findings and recommendations of the multiple studies conducted by both the Center for Education Statistics and governing board contractors. These findings were, after all, already supporting policy, guidelines, and specifications for developing public-facing reports. In turn, the memo encouraged a strong distinction between the traditional National Assessment of Educational Progress (Report Card) reports, which provide extensive statistical analysis, and the highlights report being proposed.

My memo continued, "In this context, we should acknowledge the importance of the traditional reports and express understanding of the need to present these data in technical terms and according to prescribed research standards. As we all know, these reports historically have been designed for use by the research community. In contrast, the highlights report we have in mind is designed for 'an audience of the interested general public.'"[4]

Stevens used all the experience and negotiating skills he had gained as longtime executive director of the Texas Business and Education Coalition to masterfully lead the committee to formal action on the policy. Additional committee work in later months tweaked the policy, added new components based on further work of the contracted Ogilvy firm, and more input from staffs of both the NCES and the governing board.

---

4. Charles E. Smith to board member John Stephens, memorandum, September 22, 2004.

In the end, the compromise was a success. NCES retained the right to continue its preparation and release of technical reports of assessment results; but the governing board assumed the role prescribed by law to plan and execute the initial release. This gave the board authority to determine the time, location, agenda, and presenters at the release event. It also gave the board the go-ahead to prepare a summary or highlights report written in clear, jargon-free style with attractive charts, tables, and graphics for initial release to the public. Most importantly, it ensured that the release of NAEP results would be free from partisan political influence, which was the basis for assigning this role to the board in the first place.

This debate spanned almost three years. To the outside world, it may have appeared much ado about nothing, a bureaucratic exercise. However, as I wrote in my briefing memo to Stevens, "It may very well be the most pivotal decision-making of our time with NAGB. If we are successful in producing reports that are clear, substantive, attractive, and responsive to the publics we are seeking to reach, the public understanding and acceptance of NAEP will be greatly expanded and enhanced."

And, indeed, that is what happened. We paved a pathway to take the Nation's Report Card from the backroom to Main Street.

# 6

FROM THE IVORY TOWER

TO THE BARBER SHOP

From the time of my selection as executive director of the National Assessment Governing Board in the fall of 2002 to the moment my active duty began in January 2003, I focused on defining goals, developing strategies, and setting priorities to achieve the mandate set for the Nation's Report Card by the passage of No Child Left Behind. As I searched my memory for lessons learned over four decades in high-level leadership roles in Tennessee, one recurring theme kept emerging that seemed especially relevant to the new role I would be assuming: communication strategies. I had consistently built my career successes on strong communication strategies effectively implemented.

I had learned the hard way that communicating at the top of the career ladder is much more complex than it is on the lower rungs. At the top, every word is magnified, every memo analyzed, every speech evaluated. In a society dominated by open mics, full disclosure, and information overload, the person at the top is constantly speaking and acting in a fishbowl.

So, what had I learned that might have relevance and application in my upcoming leadership role in the Nation's Report Card? In my life's experience, I had found several techniques that kept lines of communication open. Perhaps the most effective approach was one started in my first university presidency. Simple in concept but substantive in results, the "dutch treat" luncheon became a trademark of my administration. For eleven years on two different campuses, I hosted luncheons every week or two in the student cafeteria. Those luncheons were open to anyone—students, faculty, administrators, support staff, alumni, and even people off the street. No subject was off limits, and most of the time was devoted to answering questions and receiving comments from participants.

Over time, I watched with great interest the pattern of ebb and flow of the participation rates in the luncheons. Invariably, the numbers would fluctuate depending on the issues at play and the intensity of emotions regarding those issues. At times, the number of participants dropped below ten, prompting my staff to plead that the event had outlived its usefulness. I saw it differently. From my perspective, low participation was a good sign, an indication that the constituencies were generally content with our leadership efforts. My belief was affirmed occasionally when some issue would flare and cause the participation in the luncheons to expand significantly, sometimes to as many as two hundred. In any event, the luncheons proved effective in keeping lines of communication open, and they provided an early warning system to detect signs of growing discontent.

In my thirteen post-campus years as Tennessee commissioner of education and as chancellor of the Tennessee Board of Regents system of forty-six campuses, I had to modify my communication approach, but I retained its basic concept. In both of those roles, I spent the first year in office reaching out to the constituencies on their home grounds. As commissioner, I spent a full day in every one of the state's 139 school districts, starting with a breakfast and ending with an evening town hall meeting. In that time frame, I met at two-hour intervals with representative groups of students, teachers, administrators, school board members, parents, and community leaders. The format was much the same as the old "dutch treat" campus luncheons: a short opening statement followed by an open forum for questions and answers. As system chancellor, I did essentially the same thing, spending a full day on each of the forty-six campuses all across the state.

One day in early December of 2002, it dawned on me that the communication model I had built on the local campus and then at the statewide level might be modified even further to adapt it to a strategy for communicating nationwide to broaden knowledge and understanding of the Nation's Report Card and to deliver it from the backrooms of education researchers to Main Street America. Could a model that worked at the local and state level be retooled to fit a national communication strategy? I wanted to find out.

As I identified potential game plans from my home in Nashville in the fall of 2002, some nine hundred miles away Darv Winick was also focusing on the challenges that we would soon have to confront. Winick, a psychologist and career organizational consultant, had been active in Texas education politics since the early 1980s. He had played a lead role in founding the Texas Business and Education Coalition. While our experiences had occurred in two different states and in divergent ways, we found that we were on the same page when it came to what needed to be done to fulfill the mandate, promise, and opportunity that the No Child Left Behind legislation had given to the Nation's Report Card. We had to find ways to take the Report Card to Main Street America.

In addition to meeting with the governing board staff in the first week of January 2003, Winick and I met with Ray Fields, longtime assistant director for policy and research. We knew that Fields was a well-respected, seasoned professional, an effective communicator with immense knowledge of all the laws relating to the Nation's Report Card. In that first meeting, we formed early thoughts about a strategy for moving forward and quickly bonded around priority goals. Our top priority was to revamp how the results of the Nation's Report Card assessments would be reported to the American people.

The three of us were of one mind regarding the traditional

method of reporting: It had to be changed. The traditional reports were far too long and were filled with too much jargon and too many tables that only educational researchers could understand. Winick said we needed messaging that would play in our nation's barbershops. In retrospect, that first meeting with Fields set the stage and tone for a partnership that lasted throughout our time of leadership. He was well positioned by experience and intellect to guide us through what would be a complex and tough pathway that would require us to confront turf battles, address staffing issues, and develop messaging strategies. Dramatic change was on the horizon, but I left that first meeting confident that we had the top-level board support and a talented staff to get the task done.

Looking back now on those early days in DC, I still find it hard to believe that Winick, Fields, and I (three strangers to each other in the months preceding) forged such a strong partnership in a matter of just a few weeks. Temperamentally and stylistically, we approached each task with cautious but decisive thought processes that were consistently calm, cool, and collected. Our team bonding reflected mutual trust, respect, and clear communication. Perhaps that's why the anxieties that commonly confronted me in the initial stages of a new job never affected me as I settled into my leadership role with the Nation's Report Card. I slept well at night and faced each new day in those early weeks with confidence and optimism.

As each week passed in the winter of 2003, Fields proved over and over again that he knew what to do and when to do it. In the first several months, he charted an ambitious set of action steps, including face to face meetings with every key member of Congress and their staffs. Additionally, he arranged meetings with the leadership of every national association that had relevance to the Nation's Report Card. This strategy was a time-consuming but necessary initiative that provided opportunity to share what our governing board was doing to fill the role that No Child Left Behind had mandated. At the same time, from the external leadership group meetings, we gained valuable input that factored into our policymaking and implementation actions.

I soon found out that the making of the Nation's Report Card was a much more laborious, complex, and intellectually challenging task than it had appeared from the distance of the state commissioner of education office I had once occupied. As I reported to the governing board in May 2003,

> Literally scores of people—educators, researchers, psychometricians, subject-matter experts, and lay members of the public—are involved in a process that spans several years. At times, I have felt that I was operating in a time warp, simultaneously balancing the past with the future. For example, over the past few weeks, my staff and I have spent endless hours reviewing results from the 2002 reading assessment at the same time we have been initiating the process of developing the frameworks for the 2007 reading assessment.
>
> Switching from the past to the future and back again creates an environment in which concentration is essential, attention to detail is important, patience is desired, and a sense of humor is recommended.

My comments were underscored by all that was happening in 2003. We had the 2002 assessment results to release, while at the same time, the 2003 assessments were being conducted nationwide, the first to be administered under the umbrella of No Child Left Behind. That time frame guaranteed that the national spotlight would be on everything we did. To complicate matters, this was all happening during the turf battle I described previously between the governing board and the National Center for Education Statistics, the NCES. At a moment when the national profile of the Nation's Report Card had never been higher, the two agencies historically responsible for its administration were at war. Winick and I had no honeymoon break-in period. Against great odds, the show had to go on, and we had to find a way.

Winick and I were determined to fulfill the legislative mandate to revamp the National Assessment of Educational Progress (NAEP) reporting processes and produce reader-friendly reports useful to the American people. Within weeks of our arrival, we applied a full-court press to the issue. We commissioned four separate studies— three conducted by media and communications firm Hager Sharp and one by the Ogilvy public relations group. We convened focus groups. We conducted interviews with representative groups of the consumers of our reports—teachers, media education writers, school administrators, national association leaders, and public officials. We sought and provided advice and guidance in regard to the format, content, and readability of NAEP reports. We oversaw detailed analyses on media coverage of the 2003 reports to identify patterns of errors that may have been caused by inadequacies in our reports as well as in our reporting processes.

All of these efforts focused on preparing the governing board to act on the new responsibilities and authority we had been given by Congress, which had thrust the National Assessment of Educational Progress into the spotlight of a changing public arena in unprecedented ways. What had once been the sole province of a relatively small crowd of professional educators and research groups had rapidly become a mainstream interest. As the snowy winter months of 2003 gave way to the spring beauty of cherry blossoms, my staff and I could feel the winds of change everywhere we went.

The change manifested itself in a building-block effect as we moved from one group of thought leaders to another. Typically, a meeting with national association officials would lead to follow-up meetings with that association's governing board or membership group. In most cases, an initial meeting with a leadership team would open doors to a deeper dive into that interest group. For example, after an initial meeting with the executive director of the Council of

Chief State School Officers (CCSSO) in my first month in office, Fields and I received an invitation to meet with the CCSSO's board of directors, and that was followed by an invitation for me to speak to all chief state school officers at a national meeting. Over the next several months, this same evolving pattern of exposure continued. In short, the consumer base for NAEP had changed dramatically, and it was obvious that it would likely change considerably more in the years ahead. The issue at hand in 2003 was how NAEP reports should be adjusted to serve the interests and needs of this changing consumer base.

This concern about the clarity of NAEP's message was not new. Ten years earlier, in November 1993, the Widmeyer Communications Group had presented a report to the National Assessment Governing Board, the NAGB, that said reactions to NAEP had concluded that its "presentation of data was confusing and overwhelming" and needed to be simplified "to make the publications more eye-appealing and more user-friendly." The report recommended "more interpretation, executive summaries and policy statements . . . more sophisticated analysis of data."[1]

At that time, the governing board had been in its formative years. NCES had controlled the reporting processes, and the governing board had lacked the legislative authority to be responsive to the Widmeyer findings. However, the board and staff became increasingly mindful of the need for enhancement and patiently awaited the opportunity to become proactive. That moment came with the passage of No Child Left Behind. The governing board staff included the Widmeyer report in the briefing materials that Winick and I were provided in the fall of 2002. That background informa-

---

1. "Dissemination Strategies for the National Assessment of Educational Progress," The Widmeyer Group, p. 7. https://files.eric.ed.gov/fulltext /ED509381.pdf.

tion proved extremely helpful and enabled us to hit the ground running in early 2003.

Shortly after the release of the 2003 reports, Hager Sharp provided the governing board with two substantive reports on the media coverage of the releases, both in print and broadcast. As someone with a media background, I found that these reports provided valuable insight into the weaknesses of our reports and the steps that could be taken to improve them. In particular, the Hager Sharp studies aided us greatly by pointing out recurring errors in media reporting, suggesting strongly that our reports inadequately interpreted the findings of NAEP assessments. Specifically, the study found:

1. The distinction between achievement-level definitions and scale scores lacked clarity in the reports.
2. The charts and graphs too often confused readers rather than enlightening them.
3. The sections presenting disaggregation of subgroup performance fell short in providing context and interpretation.
4. The questions and data tools on the NAEP website were difficult to navigate.
5. The reports needed to explain more clearly the relationship between NAEP and the state assessments.

To address the issues, Hager Sharp recommended focus groups, structured interviews, and solicitation of professional expertise to determine what the Report Card consumers—teachers, media education writers, school administrators, national association leaders, and public officials—believed needed to be done to make the reports more responsive and useful. Hager Sharp also conducted market research to learn how NAEP users were using the data and to gauge the usefulness of the reports, which would determine what additional information key audiences believed would be valuable. My staff and I—as well as Winick and John Stevens—found few surprises in the findings and recommendations. Most importantly, they confirmed what we had believed and gave us greater confidence in taking corrective measures.[2]

The study done by the Ogilvy public relations group focused on providing professional expertise to staff and the governing board's Reporting and Dissemination Committee. It covered ways to improve the format, content, and readability of the reports, both print and web-based. How could the NAEP Highlights reports be made more useful to a lay reader? How could the summary reports better showcase the information readers most wanted to know? How could format and navigation be improved? How should state findings be presented? What information should be on the printed report's front page? What information should be highlighted online?

By interviewing report consumers, analyzing reports, and applying their own expertise, Ogilvy found that we needed a summary that "compresses an immense amount of data into manageable bites for public consumption." Our audience was the general public, a group not "necessarily trained in the nuances of average-scale scores vs. percentiles." Even educators and the media, they noted, "find many of the details of the reports difficult to digest." Both our print and web highlights were too complex and confusing. Ogilvy recommended simpler language and a clearer focus.[3]

The bottom line to these 2003 studies was that improving NAEP reports was a significant challenge and a main event that consumed hundreds of hours of staff and board review in the early months following passage of the NCLB. Everyone involved recognized the need for a new policy that would direct changes to improve the format, content, and readability of NAEP reports.

---

2. Charles E. Smith to National Assessment Governing Board, report, November 19, 2004.
3. NAEP: *Reporting Initial Results*, Internal contracted document (Ogilvy Public Relations Worldwide, July 22, 2004), 9-16.

As these studies were being conducted, John Stevens was guiding the Reporting and Dissemination Committee forward with new policies that transferred the authority for planning and executing the initial public release of NAEP reports from NCES, the National Center for Education Statistics, to the governing board. In spite of NCES officials' objections, the weight of the legislative language, the persuasiveness of Darv Winick, and the confidence the Bush administration had in Winick ruled the day.

As the governing board assumed its new responsibilities, external studies continued. In July 2004, the Ogilvy group delivered perhaps its most substantive report, noting that the new adopted policy guidelines were not functioning as stated and intended, the Highlights report needed improvement, and the NAEP web access was not user-friendly. Specifically, the NCES reports were written at a college-graduate level while the *Chicago Tribune*'s NAEP coverage was written at a twelfth-grade level. Moreover, the report advised that readers had difficulty locating information they wanted, charts lacked necessary explanations, and there were too many complex phrases and terms that assumed a technical knowledge that readers simply did not have.

After that report, we got even busier. In a paper commissioned for the governing board's twentieth anniversary in March 2009, John Stevens concisely outlined our pivotal November 2004 board actions, taken in response to the Ogilvy report.

> First, the R&D Committee brought forward an updated Policy Statement that clearly delineated the responsibilities of the Governing Board and NCES, and also addressed Part I of the Board's expanded role: Report Preparation and Content.
>
> Second, the Board also approved the Committee's recommended "Specifications for NAEP 2005 Reports," laying out very detailed descriptions that left no questions unanswered.

It also outlined detailed requirements for The Nation's Report Card website.

Third, the Board adopted the Committee's recommended "Reporting Schedule for 2005 NAEP Assessments" that covered 13 reports to be released beginning in September 2005 and continuing through Fall 2006 or Winter 2007.[4]

Stevens noted that the schedule posed an unprecedented challenge for the governing board, NCES, and their contractors who would face a slew of concerns touching on data analysis, report presentation, and release activities for assessments in math, reading, and science at the national, state, and (provisionally) urban-district levels, not to mention several special reports. Stevens also outlined two sections of the reporting policy that had broad implications for the governing board regarding the public release of results, the dissemination of reports, and outreach to government leaders and the general public.

These new sections were adopted by the board on May 20, 2005, completing a statement that included policy principles and guidelines for reporting, release, and dissemination of the national assessment results.

The adoption of these new sections formally ended the three-year debate between the governing board and NCES, a tough, consequential, internal struggle that played out largely outside the glare of the media spotlight. Resolving that struggle enabled the Nation's Report Card to become the education world's Main Street forerunner.

---

4. John H. Stevens, "Getting the Word Out about the National Assessment: Paper Commissioned for the 20th Anniversary of the National Assessment Governing Board 1988–2008" (NAGB, March 2009), 20. https://files.eric .ed.gov/fulltext/ED509381.pdf.

President Bush at signing ceremony for No Child Left Behind.

Charles Smith testifying at US Senate Education Subcommittee meeting chaired by Lamar Alexander.

National Assessment Governing Board executive director Charles Smith and Board Chairman Darvin Winick at the New Mexico governor's residence for a reception with the state's political and education leaders prior to a quarterly board meeting.

Charles Smith presides at a national press conference announcing new NAEP reports as board chair Darv Winick responds to a media question.

Board Chairman Darv Winick responds to media question at National Press Club event in Washington, DC.

Charles Smith testifying on NAEP history and civics assessments at US Senate Education Subcommittee.

Charles Smith appearing as guest on a Sunday morning special report on C-SPAN.

Historian David McCullough testifies at US Senate Education Subcommittee hearing on the status of American students' knowledge and understanding of history and civics. Charles Smith is seated behind McCullough, awaiting his turn to testify.

## Trend in fourth-grade mathematics average scores

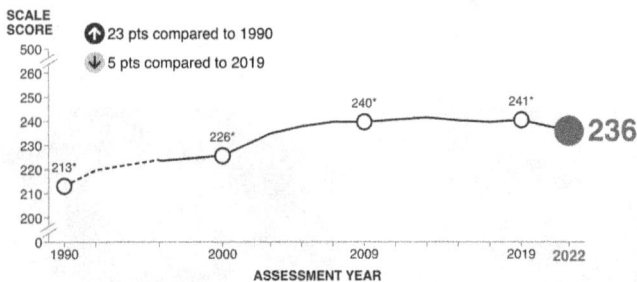

SCALE SCORE

⬆ 23 pts compared to 1990
⬇ 5 pts compared to 2019

213* (1990) · 226* (2000) · 240* (2009) · 241* (2019) · **236** (2022)

ASSESSMENT YEAR

## Trend in fourth-grade reading average scores

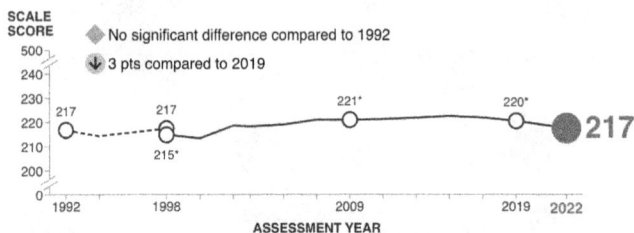

SCALE SCORE

◆ No significant difference compared to 1992
⬇ 3 pts compared to 2019

217 (1992) · 217 (1998) / 215* · 221* (2009) · 220* (2019) · **217** (2022)

ASSESSMENT YEAR

## Trend in eighth-grade mathematics average scores

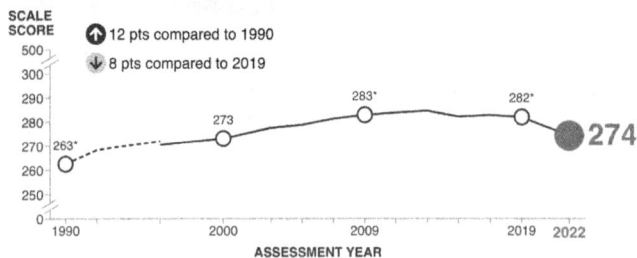

SCALE SCORE

⬆ 12 pts compared to 1990
⬇ 8 pts compared to 2019

263* (1990) · 273 (2000) · 283* (2009) · 282* (2019) · **274** (2022)

ASSESSMENT YEAR

## Trend in eighth-grade reading average scores

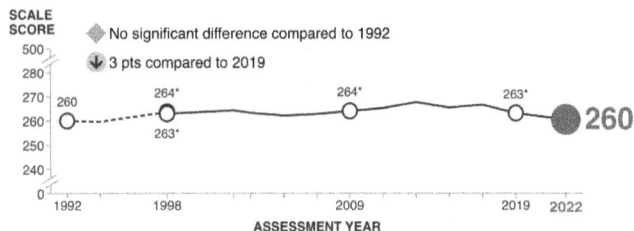

SCALE SCORE

◆ No significant difference compared to 1992
⬇ 3 pts compared to 2019

260 (1992) · 264* (1998) / 263* · 264* (2009) · 263* (2019) · **260** (2022)

ASSESSMENT YEAR

LEGEND ---- Accommodations not permitted — Accommodations permitted * Significantly different (*p*<.05) from 20

# 7

## BECOMING A BONA FIDE

## MEDIA STAR

Throughout 2003 and 2004, the governing board and its staff focused on initiatives to increase public awareness of the Nation's Report Card and worked to reshape the presentation of assessment results. We all recognized that our first real test would come with the release of the 2005 National Assessment of Educational Progress reports on student performance in reading and math. For the first time, the report would present two sets of NAEP data collected since the passage of No Child Left Behind—2003 and 2005—thus allowing a comparison of gains and losses over a two-year period in every category. Also, for the first time, state-level assessment data would be matched up with NAEP results in two different years, providing the same comparison opportunity.

We knew that the release of the Nation's Report Card in the fall of 2005 would be big news. In fact, a featured speaker at a 2005 annual meeting of the national Education Writers Association dramatically told the assembled group of education reporters that the release of the 2005 Nation's Report Card in math and reading would "clearly be the number one education news story of the year." He was right.[1]

---

1. Charles E. Smith to National Assessment Governing Board, report, August 5, 2005.

The morale of the governing board and staff had been soaring ever since the Bush administration had placed the Nation's Report Card on the front row of the national stage. I could not have signed on at a better time. We had a team prepared to seize the moment, and we did. To even a casual observer, the dramatic change in the way the governing board reported assessment results was clear and substantive. The old reports, designed primarily for the research community, became a thing of the past, replaced by reader-friendly reports with clear language, understandable tables, and relevant findings. The board's Reporting and Dissemination Committee refined and changed policies. We streamlined report release events and expanded briefing sessions with policymakers and the media.

Thanks to all of these efforts, media reporting of results dramatically improved both in accuracy and depth of coverage. Policymakers better understood what the results meant. Support for the Nation's Report Card and the governing board grew stronger. In that breakout period in media coverage, Winick and I cultivated the interest and support of several key journalists at major national newspapers and agencies, including Ben Feller, chief White House correspondent for the Associated Press, Sam Dillon, senior education writer for the *New York Times*, Greg Toppo, education reporter for *USA Today*, and the entire team of education reporters at *Education Week*. At one point early in the process, we set up basic training sessions for media representatives to give them somewhat of a primer on NAEP and the reporting process. We had some doubt about whether anyone would be interested, but the event proved popular. Feller, Dillon, and Toppo were among the journalists attending.

The governing board became aggressive in getting the story of the national assessment out to the American people. Outreach initiatives were shaped and delivered on multiple fronts. On the evening before out-of-town board meetings, we scheduled outreach dinners with the thought leaders of the city and state where we met.

We made multiple presentations to state boards of education and state legislative committees. We testified often to Congressional committees and met with editorial boards of major newspapers. The Council of Chief State School Officers partnered with us to create an Advisory Task Force. Several national associations invited us to make presentations to their boards. The governing board's multiple outreach efforts made great inroads into public understanding.

On November 18, 2003, I sent a memorandum to members of the governing board detailing three "emerging shifts in focus" noted in media coverage of the 2003 NAEP reading and mathematics assessments. A review of scores of newspapers found more attention being given to disaggregated data and less to the traditional reporting of overall averages, more prominence being given to the role of NAEP as a benchmark for evaluating performance at the state level, and more coverage being given to achievement level data and the debate surrounding the issue of standard setting. "This sampling of excerpts from news stories suggests that our efforts to secure a greater balance in the reporting of average scores and disaggregated data may be working," I wrote. "The changing nature of the content of the news coverage places a high priority on our need to speak clearly and forcefully about what NAEP is and isn't, particularly in regard to achievement level setting."[2]

The most tangible evidence that our efforts were paying off emerged unexpectedly in December 2006 when the credible Editorial Projects in Education Research Center (ERC) released a major study of the factors that had influenced the national educational policy landscape during the period from 1996 to 2006. Using a two-stage survey methodology, ERC researchers "asked leading education-policy experts first to identify and then to rate highly

---

2. Charles E. Smith to Governing Board Members, memorandum, November 18, 2003.

influential agents or 'influentials' across four different categories—
Studies, Organizations, People, and Information Sources."

The study found that the National Assessment of Educational
Progress easily outdistanced the field of nominees and achieved an
overall influence-index value of 100 points. The ERC's report noted
that NAEP earned the "perfect score by receiving top rankings for
each of the three influence elements (expert ratings, news coverage,
and citation in scholarly journals). Its performance is particularly
dominant in the areas of both news and journal citations. For example, NAEP receives more news media hits than the rest of the
studies on the short list combined."

In the study, NAEP had more than 10,000 verified hits in the
Nexis research service search, easily dominating the field of top
studies. The second-place finisher, Trends in International Mathematics and Science Study (TIMSS), had only about 1,500 citations in all. In addition to NAEP's "unparalleled level of influence
in terms of news coverage," the report noted that the EBSCO (a
leading provider of research databases) citation search found NAEP
again on top with "its 100-point score corresponding to 1,680 verified hits in peer-reviewed journals."

NAEP also topped the ratings in the study's ranking of leading information sources. The ERC report included the following
statement: "We noted that NAEP offers a depth and breadth of
information to the public in the form of statistical indicators, databases, descriptive and technical reports, research studies, on-line
data tools, and brief publications designed for the general public."
Interestingly, the study showed that NAEP outperformed *Education Week*, a widely read national print trade publication, as a top
information source.

The ERC study shed some very positive light on NAEP's expanding role as an "influential agent" on the national educational
policy landscape. It provided evidence of progress being made in
efforts to take the national assessment to Main Street America.

However, as a snapshot in time, it had to be viewed as a positive sign indicating much work on the horizon.[3]

As the prominence of NAEP expanded, another revolution of sorts was unfolding beneath the radar in all fifty states. In exchange for federal funding, No Child Left Behind mandated that every state develop standards and annually test all children in grades 3–8 in reading and mathematics. Additionally, states had to set benchmark achievement levels, using the same labels that NAEP used: Advanced, Proficient, and Basic. In the testing reporting process, data had to be disaggregated by race, ethnicity, gender, English-language proficiency, socioeconomic status, and disability. In effect, fifty little NAEPs popped up across the nation in the months following the passage of No Child Left Behind.[4]

As my staff and I, with the strong support of our governing board, crisscrossed the nation selling and promoting the Nation's Report Card, the states scrambled to meet the testing and standards mandates of NCLB. We had known from the beginning that, at some point, No Child Left Behind and the National Assessment of Educational Progress would converge—or collide. Predictably, the moment of truth began to unfold in the latter part of 2005 with the release of NAEP reading and mathematics results. For the first time, policymakers, media, and the public had national and state scores reflecting two data points: 2003 and 2005. That meant for the first time, comparisons could be made. And they were.

The designers of NCLB had known from the beginning that comparisons would create tension points. While policymakers

---

3. Christopher B. Swanson and Janelle Barlage, *Influence: A Study of the Factors Shaping Education Policy* (Editorial Projects in Education Research Center: December 2006).

4. Archived executive summary of the No Child Left Behind Act, United States Department of Education, last modified February 10, 2004. https://eric.ed.gov/fulltext/ED440373.pdf.

expected NAEP to be the reliable source by which state outcomes could be assessed, fifty states were independently setting standards and developing tests. Policymakers anticipated that the early reports would show a wide variance in results, and they were right. In the 2005 reports, the comparisons were wildly all over the board.

The most glaring discrepancies showed up in the proportion of students who were proficient in reading and mathematics at the state level compared to the NAEP findings. Most of the state reports claimed that huge majorities of their students were proficient, many of them as high as 80 to 85 percent. NAEP results typically found the Proficient rating in the same states in the 25 to 35 percent range.

As predicted, the release of the NAEP mathematics and reading scores in October 2005 became the number one national education story of the year. Practically every major daily newspaper in the nation featured the release story on page 1. Sam Dillon, senior education writer for the *New York Times*, had perhaps the best story, prominently placed on the front page. Predictably, he focused on the discrepancies between NAEP and the state assessments. Dillon wrote, "Such discrepancies have intensified the national debate over testing and accountability, with some educators saying that numerous states have created easy exams to avoid the sanctions that President Bush's centerpiece education law, No Child Left Behind, imposes on consistently low-scoring schools."

Dillon noted that in Mississippi, 89 percent of fourth graders performed at or above proficiency on state reading tests, while only 18 percent of fourth graders demonstrated proficiency on NAEP. "Oklahoma, North Carolina, Alabama, Georgia, Alaska, Texas, and more than a dozen other states all showed students doing far better on their own reading and math tests than on the federal one. . . .

"The chasm is significant because of the compromises behind the No Child Left Behind law. The law requires states to participate in the National Assessment—known to educators as NAEP—the most important federal measure of student proficiency. But in a bow to states' rights, states are allowed to use their own tests in meeting the law's central mandate—that schools increase the percentage of students demonstrating proficiency each year."[5]

Dillon wrote that Representative John A. Boehner, chairman of the House Committee on Education and the Work Force, "defended states' rights to define proficiency as they see fit and said that over time comparisons with the federal test would force them to draw up better tests. The bright lights of accountability are going to shine on the states who are kidding themselves."

My staff and our governing board shared the view expressed by Boehner. Policymakers hoped and expected that states would respond to the disparities by making their standards more NAEP-like and their assessments more rigorous. Over time, some did. But most didn't.

By mid-2006, the national media and policymakers at all levels began to focus on the disparities. The debate sharpened some six months later with the release of the 2005 NAEP science report.

The most dramatic example unfolded, actually, in my home state of Tennessee. In June 2006, I was asked to address Tennessee's NAEP 2005 results in fourth- and eighth-grade science at a standing-room-only forum at East Tennessee State University in Johnson City. Earlier that year, Tennessee had released state science test results showing more than 80 percent proficient statewide. NAEP results for that year showed less than 25 percent of Tennessee students proficient in science. The other speaker at the forum, an ACT official, reported similar disparities in proficiency in science. As soon as the session ended, the Tennessee State Board chairman Dick Ray and executive director Gary Nixon (both old friends of

---

5. Sam Dillon, "Students Ace State Tests, but earn D's from U.S.," *The New York Times*, November 26, 2005.

mine) rushed up to me and said, "Commissioner, you have given us a wake-up call. We have to make our standards more NAEP-like."

A few months later, the National Assessment Governing Board met in Nashville. During that meeting, I received an urgent call from Governor Phil Bredesen's chief policy advisor, Drew Kim, requesting a meeting that day. Less than an hour later, Drew and I were meeting at the Vanderbilt Plaza Hotel. Drew's message was that Governor Bredesen planned to announce the next day that Tennessee would be adopting standards much like NAEP, and he wanted to know as much as possible about our assessments. He said the governor also planned to launch immediately an alert to the state's business community that the first results would likely be a perceived fall off the cliff in student performance, since the standards being assessed would be significantly higher than the existing state standards.

Governor Bredesen had made an incredibly courageous move. To his credit, he stayed the course, as did his successor, Governor Haslam, and for several years the NAEP assessment results for Tennessee showed the nation's largest increase in proficiency scores. This accomplishment was no accident. Governor Bredesen's action in 2007 was quite different from that of policymakers in most other states where large disparities existed. Stated simply, many governors and state legislatures essentially ignored the evidence of disparities, an inaction that permitted my home state to be the pacesetter in gains for several years.

The disparities between NAEP and each state's own reports continued to spark considerable media attention and political debate. While some critics argued that NAEP standards were set too high, congressional support for our standards remained strong. In early 2006, noted education historian and critic Diane Ravitch chimed in on the debate with substantive commentary published in *Education Week*. She expressed the belief that the process was flawed by its reliance on states to set their own standards. "The idea that mastery of eighth-grade mathematics means one thing in Arizona and something different in Maine is absurd on its face," Ravitch wrote. She went on to say that everyone involved, from students and teachers to textbook publishers and testing agencies, should have clear content and performance standards. Ravitch concluded, "Absent national standards that command respect, as NAEP's do, standards-based reform will continue to be an empty promise."[6]

In February 2007, the US Chamber of Commerce released its first *Leaders and Laggards: A State-by-State Report Card on Educational Effectiveness.* The report relied heavily on NAEP data and focused attention on the discrepancy between NAEP reports and those of the states. Each of the fifty states received a grade on multiple factors. One of the sections noted that truth in advertising was inconsistent, specifying that "many states systematically paint a much rosier picture of how their schools are doing than is actually the case. This makes it tough for parents, voters, or business leaders to hold public officials and educators accountable."

The report locked in on Alabama. The state "reported in 2005 that 83% of its fourth graders were proficient in reading on its state test—seemingly making it one of the nation's highest performing states. But according to the National Assessment of Educational Progress (NAEP), only 22% of Alabama's fourth graders scored at or above the Proficient level on reading, making it one of the nation's poorest performing states."[7]

---

6. Diane Ravitch, "National Standards: '50 Standards for 50 States' Is a Formula for Incoherence and Obfuscation," *Education Week,* January 3, 2006.

7. *Leaders and Laggards: A State-by-State Report Card on Educational Excellence,* The Institute for a Competitive Workforce (US Chamber of Commerce, February 2007), https://www.uschamber.com/assets/archived /images/2007-_us-chamber-leaders-and-laggards.pdf.

That hard-hitting US Chamber of Commerce report attracted considerable national attention and raised even higher the national profile and credibility of the Nation's Report Card. We had arrived a bona fide media star.

But notoriety wasn't the endgame. We still needed our silver bullet.

# 8

## PAVING THE WAY

## TO MAIN STREET

In my search to find a way to simplify and communicate clearly the reporting process for the Nation's Report Card, I returned to a lesson learned as Tennessee's commissioner of education working with Governor Ned McWherter. The governor had started his career as a shoe salesman. He had learned that in order to sell a shoe, you needed to show a sample shoe. As governor, he repeatedly reminded his cabinet members that for any program we proposed to him, we needed to identify the "shoe" we would use to make the sale. He had already led by example. Early in his first campaign for governor, he had coined a simple sentence that became, in effect, a campaign slogan: "Swear me in at ten in the morning, give me four vanilla wafers and a cup of coffee, and I'll be ready to go to work."

With those few words and a box of vanilla wafers in his hand, he effectively made the point that he was prepared to be governor on day one. He would need no on-the-job training. That message became the strongest symbol of his campaign. To this day, every time I see a box of vanilla wafers, I think of McWherter.

When the governor and I unveiled his sweeping education reform initiative in 1991, our "shoe" was an old science textbook being used at that time in many of Tennessee's rural schools. We had first spotted the textbook in rural Crockett County during our statewide fact-finding tour. The governor was a bit stunned to learn that the teachers in that county—and many others—were teaching science out of a textbook that predated our nation sending a man to the moon nearly a quarter century before. Governor McWherter and I had found our sample "shoe."

That old science textbook became our constant companion as we crisscrossed the state selling our education reform plan. Rarely did we step up to a podium without the textbook in hand. At that time, it was a perfect symbol of the deficiencies that stood in the way of providing a quality education for Tennessee students.

In the early weeks of our tenure in our new roles in Washington, Darv Winick and I saw that we needed a silver bullet that would help us communicate clearly. We tried out many sample "shoes" and tested many potential choices until one shoe fit: the sample questions.

Under federal law, the National Assessment Governing Board was required to release to the public 10 percent of the questions used in each assessment, some from each of the three achievement levels we measured. As we identified our messaging challenges, it became clear that explaining the National Assessment of Educational Progress achievement levels would be our most difficult hurdle.

When Winick and I had first arrived in Washington, achievement levels had still been a relatively new component of the assessment program, a product of the 1988 law that had created the National Assessment Governing Board. One key element of the law directed the new board to identify "appropriate achievement goals . . . for each subject area" that NAEP measures. From the beginning, setting achievement levels had stirred controversy, and the end result became a game changer for a national assessment that, prior to the law change, had relied primarily on reporting average-scale scores.

Throughout the 1990s, board members and literally hundreds of subject-matter experts labored exhaustively to develop definitions, standards of measurement, and policies, which became the mechanism that allowed the NAEP, for the first time, to set expectations for what students should know and be able to do. Three levels—Basic, Proficient, and Advanced—emerged as the labels of choice for NAEP reporting, with the Proficient level being the desired goal for student achievement.

As achievement levels went public, the debate about standard-setting intensified as education and testing experts weighed in with competing viewpoints on multiple levels, including complaints that definitions were too vague, goals were unrealistic, and measurement validity was doubtful. However, Congress held strong and backed the authority of the board to set achievement levels. Then came the election of George W. Bush and his No Child Left Behind initiative, another game changer for the movement toward standards.[1]

No Child Left Behind reaffirmed the governing board's charge to establish and report achievement levels and directed that assessments in mathematics and reading at the fourth- and eighth-grade level be conducted every two years in all states. Equally significant was a mandate to all the states that they, too, establish achievement levels for state-based testing.

The new state requirement was a consequential change. Now states had to set achievement levels and report assessment results to the public and the US Department of Education every two years. Moreover, they had to use the same labels—Basic, Proficient, and Advanced—that NAEP reported. But using the same terminology created confusion and controversy, because states controlled the definitions and set the standards on their state-based testing. As a result, standards differed widely among the states, and none aligned identically with NAEP standards. So, in a growing national debate, these differentials predictably raised the profile of assessment

---

1. Maris A. Vinovskies, *Overseeing the Nation's Report Card: The Creation and Evolution of the National Assessment Governing Board* (Univ. of Michigan School of Public Policy, 1998).

standards. Media attention rose to unprecedented levels, and politicians at the state level suddenly paid attention.[2]

As noted previously, the early NAEP reports in the NCLB era showed state proficiency rates in the 25 to 40 percent range, while many states were reporting proficiency rates in the 80 to 90 percent range. Much to the chagrin of officials in many states, the huge gap between NAEP and state-set proficiency achievement raised many serious questions, attracted media attention, and confirmed a long-held belief by many political and educational leaders that states too often set their standards too low.

For the first time, the public was awakened to the reality that states too often had been lax in standard setting, and student achievement was not what it appeared to have been. In that respect, NCLB proved its value. It raised the stakes. NAEP's credibility in the world of assessment had been affirmed on a national stage.

That was the good news in my early tenure as head of the Nation's Report Card. However, the raising of NAEP's profile created new pressures to continue to produce a quality product. As stated in my first report to the board, we had no room for error now that we had been placed in the bullseye of a growing national debate.

At this point, it was time for our "shoe" to drop. We had to explain the essence of achievement levels—how they were developed, what they meant, and how best they could be used. The sample questions became the tools of choice as Winick, other board members, and I fielded questions from state governors, state boards of education, members of Congress, national associations, and media at all levels.

---

2. Archived executive summary of the No Child Left Behind Act, United States Department of Education, last modified February 10, 2004. https://georgewbush-whitehouse.archives.gov/news/reports/no-child-left-behind.html.

In the spring of 2005, Ray Fields and I had a private meeting with then Governor Mark Warner in his office at the Virginia State Capitol. Warner at that time chaired the National Governors Association. He wanted to know more about the National Assessment of Educational Progress achievement standards and how they compared to state standards across the nation. He listened carefully as Fields and I briefed him on the key aspects of NAEP, and his eyes brightened when we handed him a sample proficiency-level question from a recent NAEP assessment. We showed him the percentage of students in the national sample that had answered the question correctly compared to the percentage of Virginia students that had gotten it right. We stressed that this was just one of hundreds of sample questions available.

Warner asked multiple questions and grasped quickly the value of the sample questions in raising standards and selling achievement levels at the state level. He expressed his belief that the use of sample questions could be very helpful in convincing state political and education officials that the Proficient designation as determined by NAEP was reasonable and valid.

Fields and I left the governor's office feeling that we had secured the support of the chairman of the NGA. Within minutes after we began our journey back to our offices in DC, that feeling was confirmed by a call from the NGA executive director, who informed us that Warner had already requested that a NAEP presentation be placed on the agenda of the next meeting of the association.

Several months later, a concerned group of legislative leaders in Oklahoma invited US Chamber of Commerce officials and me to address the legislature regarding the previously referenced 2007 Chamber report entitled *Leaders and Laggards: A State-by-State Report Card on Educational Effectiveness*. The report had given several states failing grades. Oklahoma had received an "*F*" in both student achievement and truth in the state's claims about student proficiency. The chamber relied heavily on the state's results on the 2005 mandated NAEP assessments in reading and mathematics, so it was no surprise that the report had created a political firestorm in the state.

The event in Oklahoma was held on May 8, 2007. The floor of the legislative chamber was packed with members, while the galleries above were filled with media and concerned citizens. The executive vice president of the chamber outlined with specificity the reasons why the state had failed. I followed with a brief overview of NAEP, its role in the No Child Left Behind program, and the key national findings in the 2005 reports on mathematics and reading at grades 4 and 8. During my concluding remarks, I asked legislative aides to hand every legislator six sample questions from the 2005 assessment—three at grade 4 and three at grade 8. All of the questions had been pulled from the Proficient achievement level.

I acknowledged that some people thought that our Proficient designation had been set too high. Then I asked the legislators to read the sample questions with the following thought in mind: "If you had a child or grandchild at the fourth- or eighth-grade level, would you want him or her to know the answers to those six questions?"

Having testified before the Tennessee legislature hundreds of times during my many years as a commissioner of education and as chancellor of several universities, I had developed the ability to read the interest level of legislators. I immediately liked what I saw as the Oklahoma legislators read the sample questions. The legislative chamber suddenly went quiet. Every legislator focused on the questions. No one moved or looked around.

Then came the moment of truth. I asked for a show of hands of those who believed that the sample questions represented what their child or grandchild should know and be able to do. I was pleasantly surprised when practically every hand went up. I concluded my talk by simply commenting that I appreciated their affirmation that Proficient was a reasonable and appropriate goal.

The event attracted significant attention in Oklahoma's major daily newspapers. The Oklahoma City *Daily Oklahoman* published a lengthy story under a four-column headline "Why our schools got a D." The lead paragraph stated, "Oklahoma's poorly rated education system is hurting the state's business vitality, state and national business leaders said Tuesday."[3] The story included defensive statements from state education leaders, including the state schools superintendent.

Similar events took place in several other states that had received failing marks. Some of those states took corrective actions but none more effectively than my home state of Tennessee, which ultimately showed the greatest progress on NAEP assessments in the early years of this century's second decade. Meanwhile, in Oklahoma, political infighting festered, and in the US Chamber of Commerce annual reports, their results continued to earn failing marks.

Even so, the NAEP remained a crucial truth-teller in the world of education. The sample questions—our McWheteran "shoe" and silver bullet—played a key role in that success and was the final step in our six-year mission.

---

3. Jennifer Mock, "Why our schools got a D," *The Daily Oklahoman*, May 9, 2007.

# 9

## THE VALUE OF INDEPENDENCE

Prior to assuming my duties at the National Assessment Governing Board, I gave little thought to the protection from political interference that the board's creators had provided in law. From the beginning, congressional Democrats and Republicans, as well as then President Reagan, had strongly supported and protected the integrity of the Nation's Report Card. As noted in chapter 3, the Alexander/James Report made political independence of the governing board a cornerstone of its recommendations.

In the weeks leading up to my taking office on January 2, 2003, I was provided with briefing materials that reported only a couple of transgressions that had impacted the board's independence. I mentioned these previously. The first had been a relatively minor incident. A day prior to the press conference scheduled to release the NAEP findings, President George H. W. Bush privately discussed the findings during two appearances in Georgia at a private school. The second incident had happened in February 1999 and caused quite a stir inside the Beltway. The office of Vice President Al Gore, who was at that time running for president, requested that he be included in the news conference releasing the NAEP 1998 Reading results.[1]

Former Reporting and Dissemination Committee chairman

---

1. Subcommittee on Oversight and Investigations Hearing, U.S. House of Representatives, May 27, 1999, Educational Resources Information Center (ERIC), Document ED440373. https://eric.ed.gov/fulltext/ED440373.pdf.

John Stevens described the incident in a paper commissioned for the governing board's twentieth anniversary:

> The actual format of the news conference was changed shortly before the release date by the Secretary of Education, Richard Riley, who by law has final authority over the release of all Education Department reports, including those by NAEP. The news conference . . . was attended by several hundred Education Department employees and representatives of education associations.

Vice President Gore opened with a prepared statement: "Today I am proud to report to you new evidence that our efforts are beginning to pay off. For the first time, reading scores have improved for each of the three grades measured by the National Assessment of Educational Progress: fourth grade, eighth grade, and twelfth grade. This is great progress and we are proud to report it."

After Vice President Gore and most of the audience left, the event continued with a data presentation by Commissioner (Pascal) Forgione. His explanation of the results differed from that of the Vice President: "The 1998 results show some improvement in reading achievements nationally, particularly at grade 8," said Forgione. "However, the increases between 1994 and 1998 for students in grades 4 and 12 showed no net gain over the 1992 average scores." The comments by Governing Board Chairman Mark Musick were in line with the Commissioner's comments, indicating no progress from 1992 to 1998 at grades 4 and 12 and only slight gains at grade 8.[2]

---

2. John H. Stevens, "Getting the Word Out about the National Assessment: Paper Commissioned for the 20th Anniversary of the National Assessment Governing Board 1988–2008" (NAGB, March 2009), 5–6. https://files.eric.ed.gov/fulltext/ED509381.pdf.

The Gore incident stirred immediate and strong repercussions. Musick fired off a blunt letter to Commissioner Forgione expressing concern that the "format, tone, and substance of the news conference was not consistent with the principle of an independent, non-partisan release of National Assessment data, an important and long-standing board policy."[3]

Musick went on to state that the plan approved by the board had not been followed, and the arrangements had put more focus on the vice president and the administration's education policy than on the NAEP report. He commented that the presentation of the data by the commissioner had taken place toward the end of the program after the vice president had spoken and much of the audience had left. He also observed that the press had been placed in a roped-off area at the back of the room, while education association representatives and Education Department staff were at the front.

Predictably, Congress soon entered the fray, and the House Committee on Education and the Workforce called a formal hearing. In every way, the incident was a public relations nightmare and posed a serious threat to the independence and integrity of the Nation's Report Card. In the end, the governing board passed a policy transferring authority for the release of NAEP reports from the Education Department to the National Center for Education Statistics, clearly stating that henceforth the assessment results "shall be a straightforward presentation of significant data with no political commentary or program advocacy."[4] It was an ominous sign of what was to come later. (Commissioner Forgione resigned after he was advised that the White House would not be reappointing him.)

In my early weeks as executive director, I thought often about the

---

3. Ibid., p. 7.

4. Mark Musick to Subcommittee on Oversight and Investigations Committee on Education and the Workforce, U.S. House of Representatives, testimony, May 27, 1999, 3.

mandates included in the law implementing the Alexander/James Report. I saw the relevance of the political independence of the safeguards provided by the law, and I appreciated the vision of those leaders, both on the Alexander/James committee and in Congress, who had seen the dangers and shaped the protections. The National Academy of Education critique of the Alexander/James Report, impressively published along with the report, noted that "in particular, the enabling legislation for the new NAEP should clearly assure independence."[5] Rarely in my lifetime have I seen such broad-based support for a single component of legislation, but clearly political independence for the National Assessment Governing Board was a given for all involved.

Fortunately, during my six-year watch as executive director, nothing like the Gore fiasco occurred. A few situations could have become serious, but thanks to Board Chairman Winick, Education Secretary Spellings, and Senators Ted Kennedy and Lamar Alexander, the Nation's Report Card and the governing board were firmly insulated from political intrusion throughout President Bush's two terms.

They were not the only ones committed to board independence. On the eve of the release of the 2003 results of the mandated reading and mathematics assessments, the board held its quarterly meeting in Washington. I was called out of a committee meeting by a staff member, who relayed a tip: Florida governor Jeb Bush planned to announce data regarding the performance of his state's students in a public speech two hours prior to the official release at an event in DC.

Governor Bush had every reason to be proud of the positive Florida results; however, his planned speech preceding the official release would have been a violation of federal law. As soon as we

---

5. Alexander/James Study Group, p. 8.

received the tip, I called Chairman Winick out of the closed meeting of the board committee and advised him of the situation.

Winick immediately reached into his jacket pocket, grabbed his cell phone, and placed a call to Margaret Spellings, who at that time was the White House chief domestic policy aide to President Bush. Winick stressed to Spellings the seriousness of the matter and urged that Governor Bush abort his early release plan.

Spellings called back within minutes and advised Winick that Governor Bush was moving his planned speech to later in the day, after the official release of the Nation's Report Card at a Washington press conference. The quick actions of Winick and Spellings prevented a public relations gaffe and, worse, a violation of law.

For me, my staff, and the governing board, this was a clear and positive sign that the Bush administration was fully committed to supporting and protecting the integrity of the Nation's Report Card. We were also reassured that Vice President Gore's embarrassing fiasco politicizing the report would not be repeated on our watch.

At the governing board staff level, we occasionally had to confront threats from well-intentioned government bureaucrats seeking partisan favoritism. As part of our outreach program to communicate national assessment results, we always scheduled embargoed briefing sessions with Republican and Democrat congressional staffs in one room at the same time. The briefing sessions were always held the day before the official release event. On one occasion, Ray Fields and I were summoned to the office of a young Education Department staffer who had other ideas.

When we met with the young staffer, she demanded that we give priority to the Republican congressional staff by scheduling that group for a separate briefing to be followed later by a briefing for the Democrats' staff. We politely told her that such an approach would not only be a violation of protocol but would also be inconsistent with the spirit of bipartisanship that the governing board practiced.

The tension in the staffer's office increased as she pressed her case. At one point, Fields and I told her that, given the ebb and flow of election outcomes, the adoption of her request would set a bad precedent. We asked how she would feel if the Democrats took control of Congress in the next cycle and the Republicans had to wait their turn to be briefed.

She dodged the question and continued to push her demand. As the debate intensified, she bluntly asked if we fully understood what she expected us to do—and were we going to do it?

Without blinking, we advised her that we were not going to do what she was demanding. We added that if she wished to pursue the matter, perhaps she should contact the offices of Senators Alexander and Kennedy and even Secretary Spellings. With that said, the meeting ended abruptly.

Fields and I never knew whether she followed through with the senators or the secretary. In any event, we never heard from her again. The format of the embargoed briefings continued unchanged throughout the remainder of my two terms in office. Once again, the integrity and independence of the governing board and the Nation's Report Card had been upheld.

# 10

A DEFINING MOMENT

At some point in every leadership role during my half-century career, the organization I led experienced a defining moment. For the Nation's Report Card's march from the backroom to Main Street, the defining moment came on June 30, 2005. On that date, the United States Senate Subcommittee on Education and Early Childhood held a hearing to discuss Senate Bill 860, the American History Achievement Act, which sought to restore the teaching of American history and civics to its "rightful place" in the nation's schools.

Chaired by Senator Lamar Alexander, the subcommittee summoned me to testify on the status of the National Assessment Governing Board's plans for NAEP history and civics assessments. Alexander also invited David McCullough (1933–2022), arguably the most notable historian of our time, to address the importance of enhancing American students' knowledge and understanding of civics and American history. Senator Ted Kennedy, the ranking member of the committee, joined Alexander for the hearing.

By scheduling the committee hearing and identifying the witnesses, Alexander and Kennedy set the stage for this defining moment, and the timing could not have been better. For two years, my staff and I—with strong governing board participation—had aggressively pursued an agenda designed to expand awareness of the Nation's Report Card, to broaden our outreach to thought leaders throughout our nation, and to create a national sense of urgency to improve student performance.

The year 2005 promised to be a landmark opportunity for the National Assessment Governing Board. In the early months of that year, mandated NAEP reading and mathematics assessments were conducted in all fifty states. Assessment results were to be announced in the latter part of the year. For the first time since passage and implementation of the No Child Left Behind program, comparative data from 2003 and 2005 would be available to the education world and the media.

My staff and I had known for two years that 2005 would be a pivotal year for the Nation's Report Card. As one education reporter noted at the beginning of 2005, NAEP releases seemed destined to be the number one story of the year. We had little doubt that NAEP's profile would reach new national heights. However, we had a significant concern: the spotlight would primarily illuminate comparative results from the reading and mathematics assessments. Assessments of other subjects would be pushed further into the background, which would almost certainly arouse more critics arguing that NCLB, with its focus on reading and mathematics, was negatively impacting other subjects. From my perspective, the focus of Senate Bill 860 on history and civics was timely and important simply because of that criticism. The media coverage leading up to and even after the congressional hearing was extensive. The national *Education Week* probably captured best the essence of the moment with a by-lined article with the following clever lead: "'U.S. History: Our Worst Subject?' That was the catchy title of a hearing on Capitol Hill late last month. By the end of it, a panel of experts and several senators had pretty much agreed that the answer was yes."[1]

---

1. Vaishali Honawar, "History Test," *Education Week*, July 12, 2005.

In my first report to the National Assessment Governing Board in March 2003, I had sounded the alarm about the dangers of neglecting the other subjects. I had noted that by mandating state-designed and delivered tests as well as requiring that all states use the fourth- and eighth-grade NAEP assessments in reading and math, No Child Left Behind legislation may have inadvertently discouraged the continued use of other NAEP assessments by the states. I voiced concern that the pressures associated with new mandated assessments would inevitably create the temptation at the state level to cut back on non-mandated assessments such as science, history, civics, geography, and writing.

"We must be proactive in selling the notion that NAEP is a lot more than its assessments at grades 4 and 8 in reading and math," I said. "We must be aggressive in promoting the value of all of our assessments. We must be forceful in advocating that NAEP must continue to serve the whole breadth of American education and not become just a measurement of one part of it. It would be a shame to see all the 'value-added' that the No Child Left Behind initiative has provided NAEP be diminished by a decline in the use of the voluntary assessment of other subjects."[2]

Against this backdrop of emerging identity at the national level, the 2005 Senate committee hearing gave the Nation's Report Card an unexpected but welcome opportunity to make a giant leap forward in stature and impact. On June 30, the hearing room brought together several symbolic and substantive elements that advanced the cause of the Nation's Report Card. Lamar Alexander had been the primary architect of the report that led to the creation of the National Assessment Governing Board. Ted Kennedy had been the prime mover in the passage of the law that implemented the recommendations of

---

2. Charles E. Smith to National Assessment Governing Board, report, March 2003.

the Alexander report and had been a key supporter of the legislation that enacted No Child Left Behind.

The hearing also placed the Nation's Report Card onstage with the beloved historian David McCullough, who invited the assembly to reflect on the state of history and civics education as measured and reported by the Report Card. The importance of the hearing's subject cannot be overstated. Just as reports rolled out detailing NCLB's impact on reading and mathematics, the hearing called for a second spotlight on history and civics education. The label given to the event added to its significance: "U.S. History: Our Worst Subject."

My diary entry from that day notes the surreal nature of the hearing for me. I had attended many congressional events in Room SD-430 of the Dirksen Senate Office Building, but never had I testified there. When my staff and I arrived at the hearing site, we scanned the room, took note of the setting, and took our assigned seats in the first row behind the witness table. I had come into the hearing with a strong sense of confidence. My staff had prepared me well. However, I must say that I was a bit awestruck when McCullough and his entourage walked into the room through a side door and Senators Lamar Alexander and Ted Kennedy took their committee seats at the front.

Chairman Alexander opened the hearing invoking Report Card findings: "Fewer students have a basic understanding of American history than have a basic understanding of any other subject tested, including math, science, and reading. So, when you look at our national report card, American history is our worst subject." Alexander said that he and Senator Kennedy had introduced the American History Achievement Act "to put the teaching of American history and civics back in its rightful place in our school curriculum so our children can grow up learning what it means to be an American." He cited a Hart-Teeter poll of 1,300 adults that found that 26 percent of the respondents stated "producing literate, educated citizens who can participate in our democracy" should be the primary goal of education. Teaching math, reading, and writing was selected by only 15 percent, he said.[3]

McCullough, the leadoff witness and clearly the star attraction, lived up to my expectations, and judging by their attentiveness, he did not disappoint the crowd of onlookers in the packed hearing room. He passionately presented an eloquent defense of the value of American history literacy to the survival of our nation's democracy and expressed concern that No Child Left Behind's focus on reading and mathematics would potentially have a negative impact on other subjects, particularly American history.

"Now, because of the No Child Left Behind program, sadly, history is being put on the backburner or taken off the stove altogether in many schools, with the argument that we have to concentrate on reading and mathematics and science," McCullough testified. "Well, fine, to concentrate on the reading all they want. But they don't just have to read what is conventionally seen as literature. They can read the literature of history. This could bring young people and their teachers into a love of history, which is essential. If we raise generation after generation of young Americans who are historically illiterate, we are running a terrible risk for this country."[4]

McCullough cited example after example of historical literature that could be factored into the reading programs in the nation's schools. He closed his testimony by urging that educators concentrate their efforts on weaving the literature of history into reading

---

3. *U.S. History: Our Worst Subject? Hearing before the Subcommittee on Education and Early Childhood Development*, S. Hrg. 109-173, at 3-4 (June 30, 2005) (statement of Lamar Alexander, Chairman), https://www.govinfo.gov/content/pkg/CHRG-109shrg22340/pdf/CHRG-109shrg22340.pdf.

4. *U.S. History: Our Worst Subject?*, S. Hrg. 109-173, at 6 (statement of David McCullough, Historian and Author), https://www.govinfo.gov/content/pkg/CHRG-109shrg22340/pdf/CHRG-109shrg22340.pdf.

programs in elementary schools. "If you can catch [children] then, you have them for life," he said.[5]

McCullough and I had not shared texts of our testimony prior to the hearing, but his remarks could not have provided a better lead-in to my statement. My testimony confirmed with hard data McCullough's concerns about the state of history and civics education in our nation. The data put numbers on the grim picture his testimony painted.

"The student achievement results of previous NAEP assessments are cause for great concern," I testified. "What students don't know about US history and civics is significant. We have to be troubled by a finding from the 2001 US history assessment that 57 percent of twelfth graders scored below the Basic level of achievement, a percentage unchanged from the 1994 assessment. Failure to achieve Basic means that the majority of twelfth graders were unable to identify the significance of many people, places, events, dates, ideas, and documents in US history. It also means that they fail to relate relevant experience from the past in understanding contemporary issues."

I noted that in civics, the picture that emerged from the 1998 assessment was not as gloomy as that for history but was still a cause for concern. "More than a third of the twelfth graders fell below the basic level of achievement in civics," I said. "This means that more than one in three members of this nation's class of 1998, a group approaching or at voting age at the time they took the assessment, did not demonstrate an understanding of the principles of American government, its structure of checks and balances, and the role of political parties and interest groups on our democracy."[6]

---

5. Ibid., p. 10.
6. *U.S. History: Our Worst Subject?*, S. Hrg. 109-173, at 15 (statement of Charles E. Smith, Executive Director, National Assessment Governing Board), https://www.govinfo.gov/content/pkg/CHRG-109shrg22340/pdf /CHRG-109shrg22340.pdf.

At the time of the hearing, the National Assessment Governing Board had overseen only two US history assessments, in 1994 and 2001, and one civics assessment in 1998. However, in the aftermath of passage of NCLB in 2001, history and civics actually gained priority on the board's agenda. Board members shared my concern about the voluntary assessments, such as US history and civics, possibly fading away as the mandated mathematics and reading assessments rose to the forefront. Fortunately, the NAEP legislation gave the board authority to determine the schedule of subjects and grades to be assessed by NAEP. Taking this authority seriously, the board maintained a schedule of assessments with a minimum ten-year outlook to allow advance notice to NAEP participants and sufficient time to plan for NAEP operations.

When I took office as executive director in January 2003, the board's Assessment Development Committee was in the process of revising and updating the framework for the 2006 US history assessment. The board approved the revised framework at its August 2003 meeting. Two years later, just a month before Senator Alexander's hearing, the board adopted a schedule of assessments that provided for the assessment of US history and civics in grades 4, 8, and 12 every four years.

While the hearing had not yet been scheduled at the time the board met, the timing provided me the perfect opportunity to herald the significant enhancement of the focus of the Nation's Report Card on US history and civics. A month earlier, the history and civics action by the board had attracted little attention, because the media was more interested in board action on NCLB mandated assessments. In sharp contrast, the Senate hearing put history and civics front and center on a national stage. David McCullough attracted a strong audience of educators and media, and he said all the right things.

The setting was perfect, as was the timing. I knew we had hit a home run when Chairman Alexander said, "Now as I understand it, you said that the national assessment in US history and in civics—that is two different assessments, right?"

"Yes," I answered.

"One in history, one in civics," said Alexander. "And that the next national assessment is scheduled for 2006? Is that right?"

"Yes, sir," I said.

"In the fourth, eighth, and twelfth grades?"

"Yes, sir."

"And then it will be again in 2010 and 2014."

"Yes, sir," I said. "The 2006 had already been scheduled, but the change in schedule added 2010 and 2014."

"So, we can look forward, based upon your recent action, to a national assessment in 2006, 2010, 2014, in all three grades, of US history and in civics?"

"Yes, sir."

I watched Alexander's body language throughout the exchange and, having worked with him for many years in Tennessee, I felt that he was pleased. He confirmed that when he said, "Well, that is terrific."[7]

In a career that included three university chancellorships and a seven-year run as a state commissioner of education, I had logged thousands of hours of testimony before legislative committees. Never before had I felt better about the outcome of a hearing. We'd had a substantive message and, based on comments of Alexander and Kennedy's staff and other staffers at the hearing, it had been well-received by political leaders. We had taken a major step forward in signaling our board's commitment not only to protecting voluntary assessments in the time of NCLB's focus on mathematics and reading but also to expanding the voluntary assessments. I have

---

7. Ibid., pp. 85–86.

kept the transcript of that hearing and review it now and then as a reminder of a good day for the Nation's Report Card.

In 2006, the governing board did what it said it would do. It delivered US history assessments to a nationally representative sample of 29,000 students in grades 4, 8, and 12. Another 25,000 students in those grades took the civics assessment. On May 16, 2007, in Boston, the board released the results of both assessments. In history, overall achievement improved significantly from previous assessments (1994 and 2001) at all three grade levels, while student performance in civics at the fourth-grade level also showed significant gains over the previous assessment in 1998. Achievement in civics at the eighth- and twelfth-grade levels remained flat.

Consistent with our governing board's initiative to broaden the image of the Nation's Report Card, we chose the historic Boston Public Library as the site for the national press conference to announce the results of the 2006 US history and civics assessments. The event attracted a large crowd of dignitaries and national media and was one of the most successful release events we had during my time as executive director. Board chairman Darv Winick noted in his remarks at the press conference that in addition to positive trend-lines overall, the lowest performing students showed large gains in both subjects and the achievement gaps between racial and ethnic groups were closing. However, he stressed that the findings left no doubt that student performance in history and civics had a long way to go to meet our nation's needs as a democracy.

As the education world and the national media digested the results of the US history and civics assessments, we realized that the improving student performance offered evidence that the No Child Left Behind program's focus on mathematics and reading was not diminishing other subjects as many critics had predicted.

Kati Haycock, director of the respected Education Trust in Washington, DC, issued a strong statement. "These results indicate that elementary school growth in reading and mathematics has been contributing to, rather than detracting from, a student's opportunity for broad enrichment and academic success. It's a myth that concentrating extra efforts in reading and mathematics compromises achievement in other areas. Like the gains on the 2005 NAEP science test, today's results are a reminder that this argument simply doesn't hold water."[8]

Our leadership team quickly recognized the payoff being reaped from our decision in 2003 to schedule as soon as possible the science, history, and civics assessments. We had no way to know whether the assessments would yield positive or negative results, but we believed the initiative would demonstrate our commitment to keeping assessments other than mathematics and reading on the front burner. It turned out to be the right decision.

The governing board took yet another significant step to promote subjects other than mathematics and reading by scheduling NAEP's first-ever economics assessment in 2006. In preparation for the assessment, the governing board and staff applied a full-court press to ensure the inclusion of a wide range of topics and viewpoints in the economics assessment frameworks. At the event announcing the results, Chairman Winick noted that more than five hundred educators, policy makers, representatives of business and industry, and parents had participated in ten public forums to provide expert testimony. We viewed the unveiling of a new assessment as a perfect opportunity to go public with details about the complexity of the economics assessment framework development and to communicate why the process mattered. It was another important step in demystifying the Nation's Report Card and taking it to Main Street.

As a first-time assessment of student performance in the subject

---

8. Kati Haycock, Director of the Education Trust, Media Statement on 2006 National Assessment of Educational Progress in U.S. History and Civics, May 15, 2007.

of economics, the results offered no comparative data. However, it did provide a baseline from which future assessments could be compared. Seventy-nine percent of the representative sample of about 11,500 high school seniors in 590 public and private schools displayed a basic understanding of economics.

Bottom line, by 2007 the National Assessment Governing Board had achieved its twin goals of introducing the NCLB-mandated, every-other-year assessments of fourth and eighth graders in mathematics and reading as well as weaving assessments of history, civics, and economics into the regular, recurring schedule. Now the board had the challenge of fulfilling the promise of future assessments.

The presidency of George W. Bush ended on January 20, 2009, but the independent National Assessment Governing Board moved ahead with all previously scheduled 2009 assessments—mathematics, reading, and science in grades 4, 8, and 12. In 2010, national assessments were conducted in US history, civics, and geography at grades 4, 8, and 12.

The releases of all six reports occurred after both Chairman Winick's term and mine had expired, but I watched with great interest and studied carefully the results. I was pleased to see that the foundation that had been built during our time of leadership stood firm and strong. Commitments had been fulfilled. By focusing on assessments in subjects such as US history, civics, science, and economics, we had softened the criticism of NCLB's mandates for assessments in mathematics and science and had provided evidence that student performance in the other subjects had not been adversely affected. Clearly, it had been a defining moment for the Nation's Report Card.

# 11

## A PROFILE IN COURAGE

In 2002, as the Bush administration began implementation of No Child Left Behind and the governing board geared up to provide the mandated assessment schedule required by the new law, a related initiative quietly moved forward beneath the radar, expertly guided by a soft-spoken but courageous national association leader by the name of Michael Casserly, executive director of the Council of the Great City Schools, whose membership at that time included sixty-five of the largest urban school districts in the nation. What Casserly and the leadership of the participating districts did to support the initiative changed forever the image of our nation's urban schools and played a significant role in the governing board's goal to take the Nation's Report Card from the backroom to Main Street.

Stated simply, Casserly and the participating districts wanted a NAEP sample size large enough to ensure that their results could be reported and compared. They wanted urban schools to be permitted to do voluntarily what states were required to do under No Child Left Behind—participate every other year in the Nation's Report Card reading and mathematics assessments in grades 4 and 8. Casserly backed up his wishes by almost singlehandedly securing Congressional support for funding in 2002. His actions were revolutionary and consequential.

Casserly's strong support helped establish the Trial Urban District Assessment, or TUDA, as a regular part of NAEP program.

As a result, urban school districts, long maligned for perceived weaknesses, voluntarily placed themselves—for the first time—on the frontline of national scrutiny. Casserly, working in concert with NAEP officials, succeeded in securing congressional support for the participation of six urban school districts in the 2002 national and state assessment process. Significantly, the Council had more than enough willing districts to fill the voluntary slots. In that first year of TUDA, fourth- and eighth-grade students in the districts of Atlanta, Chicago, District of Columbia, Houston, Los Angeles, and New York City participated along with students from across the states in reading and writing assessments.

The results of the first round of assessments contained few surprises. In all six districts, students' overall performance in most categories was lower than the national average. However, our emerging reports of disaggregated data disclosed multiple nuggets of positive news. For example, the report showed that in reading and writing, White fourth graders in Atlanta and the District of Columbia scored significantly higher than the national average for Whites in both average scores and percentages at or above Proficient. At the same time, the results also showed glaring gaps in achievement between White and minority students, putting a spotlight on the need for effective intervention.[1]

In my remarks at the media event in July 2003, I praised Casserly and the participating urban districts for their courage in putting their performance on the line. I noted that the first round of data would serve the districts as a benchmark for studying changes in performance of representative samples of their students and of particular subgroups. "Clearly, the urban districts have a huge challenge

---

1. *National Assessment Governing Board 2002 Trial Urban District Assessment (TUDA) in Mathematics and Reading Report* (NAGB, July 10, 2003), www.nagb.gov.

in bringing student performance to acceptable standards," I said. "However, the willingness of school district leaders and the Council of the Great City Schools to put their schools on the line with NAEP is a clear signal that they are serious in their efforts to be accountable and strongly committed to improving achievement."[2]

Six months later, the governing board released the 2003 Trial Urban District Assessment results in reading and mathematics in the original six urban districts, plus four new ones—Boston, Charlotte-Mecklenburg, Cleveland, and San Diego. Thanks to Casserly's vision, courage, and tenacity, the foundation for TUDA had been laid. The 2002 and 2003 assessments had demonstrated the viability of TUDA. Consequently, the governing board included it as an integral part of the assessment schedule it set for the Nation's Report Card.

Darv Winick and I developed a strong friendship with Casserly. Among people who worked with national associations related to education, he stood tall as a doer who truly cared about quality education. His interest in the national assessment did not end when the results were announced. For him, that was the beginning. Impressively, he and his staff spent endless hours analyzing the results of the TUDA assessments, identifying strengths and weaknesses. They formed what Casserly called educational SWAT teams made up of school officials from across the country who would go into participating urban districts for several days of intensive review of findings and make recommendations for improvements.

During my six years as executive director, Casserly and I spent many hours together discussing assessment results and comparing notes about what seemed to work in educational improvement

---

2. Charles E. Smith, Prepared Remarks at Media Event Announcing the Results of 2002 TUDA Assessments in Mathematics and Reading, July 10, 2003.

efforts. As we traveled around the country to meet with newspaper editorial boards, visit with urban school officials, and share the podium at public events, I consistently saw the missionary zeal he exhibited in all that he did.

In 2006, Dr. Beverly Hall (1946–2015), superintendent of the Atlanta Public Schools, contacted Casserly and me with concerns about the TUDA program. Dr. Hall had become extremely frustrated by the negative local media coverage of the national assessment results in her district. She expressed concern about her inability to understand the national assessment adequately enough to explain the results to the media. In particular, she noted a concern that the reports we were releasing each assessment cycle did not reflect some key areas where the Atlanta system was making significant improvement. For example, our tables in the reports did not pick up the dramatic improvement that the Atlanta system showed in moving students from the Below Basic category closer to the Basic level. Also, some of the science items on the fourth-grade assessment covered material that was not taught until the fifth grade in the Georgia state mandated curriculum. These concerns had reached a level that caused Dr. Hall to lean toward withdrawing from the TUDA program.

Casserly and I responded quickly. We volunteered to go with Dr. Hall to meet with the *Atlanta Journal-Constitution* editorial board on the day before the release of the 2005 TUDA science assessment results. In concert with the National Center for Education Statistics we agreed to revise the tables in our reports to capture the type of movement that was occurring in Atlanta. NCES agreed to add a full-time TUDA coordinator at the State Services Center of the National Assessment of Educational Progress.

Dr. Hall, Casserly, and I set up a meeting with the *Atlanta Journal-Constitution* editorial board, which was generous with the time they allotted us and seemed genuinely interested in what we had to say. Casserly and I took time to lay out in some detail the history of

TUDA, including mention that Atlanta was one of the first urban systems to volunteer to participate. We put the Atlanta scores in the context of all the TUDA participants and shared disaggregated data. We also noted the concern Dr. Hall had shared with us about our reporting charts failing to show where Atlanta was making its greatest gains: in the number of students nearing the Basic level.

Casserly and I laid out examples where curriculum alignment was out of sync with the national assessment, including the reference Dr. Hall had made about a section of the fourth-grade assessment that covered information that Atlanta students would not learn until the fifth grade. And Casserly explained ways in which the Council of the Great City Schools was using TUDA results to pinpoint instructional weaknesses and identify remedies. To our surprise (and dismay), the editorial board members had not been aware of most of what we shared.

That meeting resulted in a lengthy front-page story on the day after the national media release. It was a fair story, reporting accurately the results and putting into context the demographic realities of the urban schools participating in TUDA. A few days later, the *Atlanta Journal-Constitution* published a positive editorial that praised the Atlanta system for volunteering to participate in TUDA, gave context to where Atlanta stood in comparison to other urban systems, and noted issues such as the Georgia standards in science being out of sync with some of the items on the national assessment. In large measure, the editorial reflected all we had shared in the editorial board meeting.[3]

---

3. Patti Ghezzi, "Atlanta Schools in Science; Eighth Graders Lowest in 10 Cities," *The Atlanta Journal-Constitution*, November 16, 2006; and Maureen Downey, "Our Opinions: Science Pushed Aside; Focus on Math and Reading Leaves Another Key Subject on Back Burner, and Test Results Reflect That," *The Atlanta Journal-Constitution*, November 20, 2006.

Dr. Hall was pleased with the media coverage and stayed the course with TUDA, as have her successors. Casserly and I left Atlanta with a sense of the challenge we faced to help the media and public to better understand the Nation's Report Card.

As the waiting list of willing urban systems grew, Casserly continued his push for more funding for additional participants. By the time my second term as executive director ended in 2008, the number of urban systems in TUDA had grown to eleven. By 2018, that number had increased to twenty-seven, a testament to Casserly's ability to secure funding from Congress, the willingness of urban systems to put their students' performance on the line in public, and the governing board's commitment and support for reporting on a critical segment of education in the US.

At the 2018 media release event announcing the results of the 2017 assessments, I read Casserly's comments with great interest. He said,

Remember that we started this initiative to help us in three ways: One, we—as urban school systems—wanted to demonstrate that we were fully committed to the highest academic standards for our children.

Two, we wanted to be able to compare ourselves with those that share many of the same challenges and serve similar populations of students who are disproportionately poorer, likely to have faced discrimination, are English learners, and students with disabilities.

Finally, we wanted a way to gauge our progress and evaluate our reforms in ways that the current fifty-state assessment system does not allow.

These NAEP data give us the tools we need to ask hard questions about our instructional practices and where we need to improve. And the results are giving us even greater confidence that urban education in this nation can be substantially improved.[4]

The 2017 TUDA assessment represented the ninth time since 2002 that a coalition of urban school districts had taken the National Assessment of Educational Progress. The results reflected all that Casserly had expressed and hoped for when the program began. Between 2002 and 2017, large city schools improved their fourth-grade reading performance on NAEP by eleven scale-score points and narrowed the gap between urban schools and the national public sample by 48.3 percent. At the eighth-grade level, urban reading scores on NAEP improved nearly eight points since 2002 and narrowed the gap with the national public sample by about 41 percent. In math, the urban schools gained 7.5 scale-score points in the fourth grade between 2003 and 2017 and narrowed the gap with the national public sample by 24 percent. At the eighth-grade level in math, urban schools gained twelve points and narrowed the gap with the national public sample by 45.8 percent. In all, gains of urban schools have risen significantly faster than the national public sample over the last fifteen years or so.[5]

The progress being made by urban schools is no real surprise to me. From the day I met Casserly, I sensed that his commitment to school improvement was uncompromising. He knew what he wanted to do and did it. However, I have no doubt that Casserly will never be content. In my judgment, Mike Casserly has earned the MVP award for promotion and proper use of the Nation's Report Card. For sure, during my six years as executive director, no one

---

4. Mike Casserly, Text of Prepared Remarks at the 2017 TUDA Data Press Conference, Council of the Great City Schools, April 10, 2018.
5. Ibid.

outside our official governing board family did more than Casserly to support our efforts to take the Nation's Report Card from the backroom to Main Street. He was clearly a profile in courage. After twenty-nine years as executive director of the council, Casserly retired in December 2020, but his legacy lives on.

# 12

## FINDING AND REPORTING

## MEANING IN

## ASSESSMENT RESULTS

As a state commissioner of education in Tennessee in the late 1980s and early '90s, I and my staff put in place a new student assessment program and created a report card process. My background in journalism had prepared me for the task of reporting meaningful and usable information to the public. So upon arrival in DC, I thought I was ready to do the same with the Nation's Report Card. However, I found quickly that the learning curve was very steep. The national assessment was much more complex than the assessments developed during my time as state commissioner. Such was the case in every state.

Test development for the Nation's Report Card was much more sophisticated, time consuming, and costly than at the state level. Administering the assessment was much more labor intensive and intricate in design. And reporting results—always a difficult task— became even more difficult as a result of No Child Left Behind.

Any public release of results had always headlined average scores and highlighted trend lines, but now the mandate of No Child Left Behind added several layers to the reporting process. In addition to reporting results for the student population as a whole, NCLB required state tests and the National Assessment of Educational

Progress to report scores of subgroups of students, including English learners, students in special education, racial minorities, and children from low-income families. Moreover, achievement levels had to be defined and reported. The National Assessment Governing Board was ready for that challenge, but most states were not.

For the first time, the law of the land dictated that the American people had a right to see disaggregated data that previously had been hidden beneath overall averages of student populations as a whole. The governing board had put achievement levels in place and had defined them, but reporting those levels to an American public unfamiliar with such levels posed a special problem. To meet the challenge, the board would have to devise new ways of reporting and develop meaningful tables and charts.

As the executive director of the board, I welcomed the challenge to present disaggregated results. In Tennessee when I was state commissioner of education, I'd had a hand in implementing the value-added model of assessment developed by University of Tennessee professor Bill Sanders. That model, controversial at the beginning, enabled school systems to measure teacher effect on student advancement on an annual basis.

The governor and I had been skeptical at first and had rejected the Sanders model in our legislative reform package, but a persistent Sanders was able to convince the legislature to amend our package and add his model. In my many discussions with Sanders, I told him that one of my concerns was that the same five or six school systems—all wealthy communities—had the highest average scores in the state year after year. I promised him that if his model disaggregated the results in a way that displayed some separation among those systems, I would believe in his approach.

In the first year in which we could compare two years of data, the results showed that one of the traditionally top school systems in average scores remained among the top performers, but one of the top five dropped all the way to 134th out of 139. The explanation was that the wealthy system that dropped to the bottom was failing to advance its students through the schooling process.

The point is that, as state commissioner, I had enthusiastically supported the Bush plan to disaggregate the data provided by the national assessment. I had viewed NAEP as a much more sophisticated approach than what we were trying to do at the state level. Time proved that to be the case.

The mandate to report disaggregated data became a game changer in the world of student assessments—a change that has become the expected norm for reporting assessment results. The change has had significant impact on the education community at every level and provided new meaning in the interpreting of assessment results.

Sean Reardon, a researcher and professor at the Stanford Graduate School of Education, succinctly summed up the value of disaggregation with these words published in a NAGB research report: "NAEP's disaggregation by race and ethnicity and (free or reduced-priced) lunch eligibility has been key to our work and lots of other people's work. They've let us compare patterns of achievement and how they relate to school, district, and state level factors. That helps us learn about how we might improve equity of outcomes."[1]

But there was another challenge in reporting results under No Child Left Behind: explaining the difference between statistically significant and educationally meaningful changes over time. From its beginning, the National Assessment of Educational Progress had focused on giving the nation a way to measure whether trendlines were up or down. The Nation's Report Card did just that. However, as the visibility of national results moved from the

---

1. *Leveraging NAEP Data to Study and Improve Education Equity: A National Assessment Governing Board Report* (NAGB, 2022), 2, www.nagb.gov.

province of educational researchers in the back rooms of think tanks to state-level boardrooms, newsrooms of mainstream media, and Main Street, the reporting task became more difficult. Early in my time as board executive director, I learned the difficulty of trying to explain that, for example, a one-point gain was significant and was meaningful as a measure of progress over time. The technical answer is complex and difficult to understand as a layman but, stated simply, the NAEP approach is similar to political polling. Pollsters that sample large groups of people produce results that contain a very small margin of error; conversely, they likely will get a large measure of error when the sample is small. In like manner, NAEP's national assessments sample tens of thousands of students and produce very small margins of error, while at the state level small subgroups of students assessed tend to produce error margins quite large.

The moment of truth in regard to trying to explain statistically significant confronted me on national television on the evening of October 19, 2005. Earlier that day, the governing board had released the results of the 2004 national assessment of reading and mathematics achievement of fourth and eighth graders. The report showed that student achievement had continued to rise, with Black, Hispanic, and lower income students making some of the larger gains. Based on national averages, achievement in mathematics had risen to its highest level in fifteen years, with most of the gains for both students in grades 4 and 8 occurring since 2000. Those gains were significant.

At the release event in Washington, governing board chairman Darv Winick had said, "These results indicate progress. The results are similar to those from the national, long-term trend assessments of nine- and thirteen-year-old students, which NAGB released last July. Parents and educators should be pleased with recent successes, especially at the elementary level. While still large, the differences between those students classified as eligible and not eligible for subsidized lunches continue to shrink."[2]

That evening, I appeared on CNN's Lou Dobbs program. He was in New York; I was in CNN's Washington headquarters near my office. The setting was a bit ominous as I was seated in a darkened studio with a single spotlight shining on me. Since I was to be the last person interviewed, I sat silently in the dark for almost an hour watching Dobbs interview a host of other people on a variety of subjects.

When my turn came, I did not have to wait long to see Dobbs's interviewing skills up close and personal. He opened the interview by describing our report as "sobering" and "showing little improvement" in test scores. He further noted that the report showed "no progress in the reading skills of fourth and eighth graders" and that math scores were "up slightly." Then came the "gotcha" curve ball. With a graph of the results of the eighth-grade math assessment (the only one showing no improvement) displayed on the screen, he noted that President Bush had "called this report encouraging." All this time, I sat there watching.

Then came the opening question: "Charles, do you agree with President Bush?"

Fortunately, I was able to keep my composure. I dodged the direct question and answered, "Well, Lou, I see some very positive points in this report, specifically the gain in scores that we're seeing in mathematics that continue as a trend that has accelerated over the past five or six years—very positive developments. In reading at the fourth-grade level, we've seen some gains in this decade that are

---

2. Darv Winick, Prepared Statement at Media Event Announcing NAEP Results on 2004 Mathematics and Reading Assessments, October 19, 2005, Washington, DC.

impressive—not as impressive as math but certainly moving in the right direction. Our concern would be with reading at the eighth-grade level, where we have not seen any particular gain in the scores.

"I think also one element that needs to be brought out here is that the gaps between the white students and the minorities in our nation continue to close, and this report shows that very clearly. And these gains are occurring at a time when the demographic shift in our nation's population is rather dramatic."

Dobbs acknowledged that my comments made "an excellent point," but he clearly was on another page in his interpretation of the findings. "If we could, I'd like to put up a chart of these gains that we're talking about here," he said. "Those are the gains in terms of reading for the fourth grade. Reading for the fourth grade, in point of fact, is not really that much of an improvement. It's one point higher, in point of fact, this year than it was in 2003. I find it—if I may say, Charles—difficult to get excited about that. It's not deteriorating; that's the good news, it seems to me. How are we going to get excited about this as improvement?"

My response focused on sampling size and processes, acknowledging that a one-point increase may appear small but emphasizing that one point was "statistically significant given the size of the sample. We assessed about 660,000 students across the nation. And the margin of error, obviously, is lessened with that large a sample, and even a 1 percent gain is considered to be significant."

I stressed to Dobbs that the real value of the National Assessment of Educational Progress came in providing data to measure progress over time. "Lou, the national assessment gives state officials in particular, and federal officials, too, a second opinion beyond the state assessments whereby they can gauge where there may be strengths and where there may be weaknesses. Our assessment is not designed to measure cause and effect. So we're not in the position to speak with authority on the basis of this assessment as to what the cause of the gains or the losses may be, but we do think the information is very valuable."

The interview ended with Dobbs stating, "And we agree with you, and we thank you for being here to share it. The measurement is absolutely critical and necessary. We thank you."

I left the interview less than pleased with the way I had handled the answers. In fact, I second-guessed myself for days. The interview, playing out on a national stage, had been a dramatic example of the difficulty of effectively communicating and interpreting the data provided in the national assessment results. Board chairman Darv Winick and others on the board thought the interview went well in view of Dobbs' persistent negative line of questioning, but they agreed with me that it revealed a weak spot: we needed a ready store of sound bites that would emphasize trend lines over time and lend weight to the idea of "statistical significance."

I had taped the interview and obtained a transcript of the program, which I used as Exhibit A of the challenge before our governing board in the age of No Child Left Behind. The lessons that I and my staff learned from that experience helped us refine our reporting processes in the months ahead.[3]

---

3. Charles E. Smith, interview by Lou Dobbs, *Lou Dobbs Tonight*, CNN, October 19, 2005, www.cnn.com/transcripts.

# 13

## AND THEN THERE

## WAS COMMON CORE

I think often of my early days as executive director and the impressions I had from the beginning that I had signed on to something special. The potential to make a big difference as a leader was clear and obvious. For six wonderful years, I and my team did our job and fulfilled the promise to make the Nation's Report Card more reader-friendly and to move it to Main Street America. So, to me, the important question is: What are the lessons learned from my experience with the Nation's Report Card in the time of George Bush's No Child Left Behind? That question has been on my mind from the day my two terms ended as the National Assessment Governing Board's executive director in 2008. I have focused often on the actions and events chronicled in these pages. In many ways, my time in DC was a magical experience, a rare moment with the opportunity of a lifetime to make a consequential difference in a high-profile setting.

Perhaps the most important lesson learned is that in order to succeed, any assessment of educational performance must have the respect and trust of its consumers, particularly those in the world of education. For more than five decades, the Nation's Report Card has earned that respect and trust in spades and has been widely acclaimed by educators, media, and political leaders as the gold standard of assessment. Achieving respect and trust was no accident but was earned over several years by educational and political leaders who supported, nurtured, and protected the Nation's Report Card.

Four important factors provided the foundation for the stability of the Nation's Report Card and the success in building and sustaining trust and respect:

1. A strong grassroots governance structure
2. Insulation from political interference
3. A sophisticated assessment design process
4. A focus on state rather than student performance

As noted previously, the National Assessment of Educational Progress governance structure is truly unique. The National Center for Education Statistics within the US Department of Education is responsible for the technical design of the assessment, the National Assessment Governing Board sets policy and controls reporting results to the public, and multiple independent contractors are delegated the responsibility of delivering a credible assessment product.

The key component in the shared governance system is the National Assessment Governing Board, which is also unique in its structure and composition. Also, unlike most boards in a political environment, its work is insulated from political interference. Its creators designed an elaborate selection process that for more than three decades has produced grassroots board members representing every major component of the education world. NAGB stands front and center as the poster child for a governing board that works in a political environment, and it has stood the test of time, providing an important example for anyone interested in creating an effective, independent board to support government, particularly in Washington, DC.

The longevity (and success) of the NAGB is underscored by the failure of the Common Core initiative that followed in the years immediately after George Bush left office. Ironically, it was the move of the Nation's Report Card from the backroom to Main Street that prompted, in large measure, the Common Core effort. Concerned by the large variance between the performance standard setting of the Nation's Report Card and that of most states, the National Governors Association and Council of Chief State School Officers (CCSSO) launched the Common Core movement in a good faith effort that was urgently needed in order to restore credibility at the state level in the assessment of school performance.

In the early days of the Common Core initiative, I had a seat at the planning table. I saw up close that the NGA and the CCSSO leaders were sincere. They were committed to improving student performance and reducing the gap between NAEP and state test findings that NCLB had exposed during the Bush administration. The Common Core leaders expressed a vision to create NAEP-like standards for adoption by the states and set general alignment with NAEP as the target. Key leaders of the NGA and CCSSO put together a small team of assessment experts to develop a game plan, and in the beginning, the initiative looked promising.

However, within months, the Common Core movement began to take on extra baggage and lose its way. The new secretary of education, Arne Duncan, unveiled a Race to the Top initiative that was well-intentioned but misguided. It put $4 billion on the table as an incentive to states to raise standards. Ultimately, the funding led to two separate consortia being created to develop Common Core standards. No one seemed to notice the contradiction in two separate national groups working to create a Common Core. That was just the first of many missteps taken by the leaders of the movement.

In short order, politicians at all levels began to weigh in. Some sought to link teacher evaluations with Common Core assessment results. Some alleged that Common Core was seeking to create a national curriculum. At the same time, the large major testing companies, sensing, logically, that a huge new assessment market might be opening up, set their sights on gaining a foothold in—if not outright control of—Common Core development. It became a train wreck in the making.

Gene Wilhoit, arguably the chief architect of the Common Core initiative and then-head of the national Council of Chief State School Officers, acknowledged in a candid interview after retiring from the CCSSO leadership post that politics disrupted the effort to make the Common Core work. "When I took over as the head of the CCSSO, I decided to make the development of these standards the keystone of my administration," he said.

> The states had to do it. Many people were concerned that if we did not do it, the federal government would. And we did not want that to happen. So the states took the lead. In fact, we told top federal government officials at the time that this was a state agenda, and we didn't want them involved in any way.
>
> There is, of course, an irony in this. Even though we were very diligent about not involving the federal government in the development of the standards, and even though we warned the federal government about doing anything that might imply federal government pressure to adopt them, the federal government still, in the Race to the Top program, created very strong incentives for the states to adopt the Common Core, and that has turned out to be enough to turn the Common Core into a political football.[1]

Thus, the initial good intent of NGA and CCSSO eventually evaporated in a haze of controversy. As the second decade of the

---

1. Gene Wilhoit, interview by Marc Tucker, National Center on Education and the Economy (cross-posted at *Education Week* and NCEE Newsletter), January 8, 2015, https://ncee.org/quick-read/gene-wilhoit-on-the -common-core-part-1/.

century neared an end, the *New York Times* captured in a December 2019 headline the essence of the elusive question: "After 10 Years of Hopes and Setbacks, What Happened to the Common Core?" What-might-have-been never became a reality.[2]

Why? The short answer is that those involved either forgot or never recognized the lessons that the successful Nation's Report Card offered them. As a result, the Common Core failure stands as exhibit A of the way not to develop an assessment program. The Nation's Report Card has an operational structure with checks and balances to ensure the quality and integrity of the assessment. The Common Core never did. The Report Card earned the trust, respect, and support of educators, political leaders, and the media. The Common Core never had a chance to achieve the same. The Report Card has a carefully designed governing board with broad grassroots representation. The Common Core governance fragmented early in the development process and lost its sense of direction. The Report Card has consistently been insulated from political interference. The Common Core became a political football. The Report Card remained true to its original purpose to measure educational progress over time with the intent to identify strengths and weaknesses in our nation's schools. The Common Core became a tool to be used punitively in teacher and student evaluation. Bottom line, we failed to heed the lessons of the Nation's Report Card.

What if the National Governors Association and the Council of Chief State School Officers had established an independent governing body like the National Assessment Governing Board? What if they had built guardrails to prevent political interference? What if they had resisted the movement to use assessment results in a punitive manner? What if they had created safeguards to protect

2. Dana Goldstein, "After 10 Years of Hopes and Setbacks, What Happened to the Common Core," *The New York Times*, December 6, 2019.

a governing board from the ever-changing political leadership spawned by the election process? Our country will never know the answers to those and many other what ifs. However, the Nation's Report Card is still standing strong, and the lessons it offers are clear and ever present.

In retrospect, Bush's decision to go with the National Assessment of Educational Progress rather than design a brand-new assessment may have been the most important judgment he made in the No Child Left Behind initiative. He went with the tried and true—an assessment well respected and trusted by the education community and Congress. That judgment stands in sharp contrast to the decision the framers of the Common Core program made during the Obama administration when they chose to create a new assessment with no history, no earned reputation, and no measure of reliability. Their initiative ultimately collapsed under the weight of political interference, ideological conflict, and dysfunctional governance.

Bush and his team took another crucial step that became a difference maker. They purposely separated the Nation's Report Card from the NCLB program itself. The governing board had primary responsibility for policy making and oversight related to the Report Card. The US Department of Education had jurisdiction over all aspects of NCLB. The importance of that separation cannot be overstated. Education reform at any level of government is almost certain to be controversial. A national reform as bold as NCLB would from day one have a huge target on its back. Thankfully, the Bush team had the forethought to shield the Nation's Report Card from the "noise" of those who resisted and criticized NCLB. That separation made it possible for the Nation's Report Card to stay aloof and out of the battle over the NCLB program. We did what we were assigned to do—be the "truth teller" in measuring educational achievement and setting standards.

Was No Child Left Behind a success or a failure? That question will be widely debated long into the future. Our nation may never have a certain answer. However, one fact is indisputable: The Nation's Report Card shows clearly that during the Bush years, student performance in reading and mathematics significantly improved, and the gaps in performance between White and Black students and White and Hispanic students closed. Did No Child Left Behind make the difference?[3] From a programmatic perspective, the jury is still out. As noted earlier, the Nation's Report Card was never designed to show cause and effect. Its purpose is to inform the public about academic achievement of elementary and secondary students over time, and it has done so with precision.

3. *2019 NAEP Mathematics and Reading Assessments: Highlighted Results at Grades 4 and 8 for the Nation, States, and Districts,* www.nationsreport card.gov/highlights/mathematics/2019 and www.nationsreportcard.gov /highlights/reading/2019.

# 14

## LEGACY

My two terms as executive director of the National Assessment Governing Board ended in August 2008, just a few months prior to the end of the Bush presidency. I left the federal government with a good feeling, knowing that the Nation's Report Card had fulfilled its promise as a reputable barometer of academic achievement during the presidency of George W. Bush. At the same time, my team and I took pride in the fact that we had taken the Nation's Report Card from the backrooms of think tanks to Main Street America. By doing so, we became a stimulus for meaningful education improvement in states and cities throughout the nation.

Rarely a day passes that I don't remember my time in Washington. I often think about that late-night Delta airlines flight on January 1, 2003—a trip that took me from the comfort of my home and family to the unknown terrain of the federal government. I remember well the mix of apprehension and excitement that filled my thoughts that night. I recall my concern that the move would unsettle my close-knit family. Time proved that concern totally unfounded. In fact, the move brought my family closer together, and DC opened the door to new experiences for my wife, Shawna Lea, our children, their spouses, and our five grandchildren.

Shawna Lea divided her time between our home in Nashville and our condo in Alexandria. We spent most every weekend together either in Tennessee or Virginia. She relished our visits to the Kennedy Center for Broadway plays and symphony performances, frequent tours of the many museums in DC, and occasional Amtrak trips to New York City. Our children and their families visited us frequently and enjoyed all the sights that the nation's capital had to offer. Their favorites were the Washington Nationals baseball games and the Washington Wizards basketball games. One grandson, Ben, actually visited nineteen times, sometimes in the summer staying two weeks at a time. He attended more than a dozen Nationals games and enjoyed many dinners at the City Club near the White House.

All of my grandchildren participated in sports, and much to my surprise and delight, I was able to attend the majority of their games. I surprised grandson Blake one mid-weeknight when he started his first high school basketball game. I flew in on a late afternoon Southwest Airlines flight that put me in Nashville forty-five minutes before the start of the game. Unfortunately, I had to fly out at 5:30 the next morning. Needless to say, I didn't get much sleep, but my grandson has never forgotten that I made his game. In short, the Washington experience added value to my entire family and gave me a strong support base that enabled me to do my job with the Nation's Report Card.

Four reporting cycles occurred during my time as executive director. In that period, scores in fourth-grade mathematics increased from 226 to 240, while eighth-grade scores rose from 273 to 283. In reading, fourth graders improved from 215 to 221, while eighth-grade performance rose from 263 to 264. In the same time frame, performance gaps between White and Black students and White and Hispanic students closed significantly, the central hope and goal of Bush's No Child Left Behind initiative. From the beginning, Bush had strongly advocated the need for disaggregated data that displayed the gaps in learning across the nation. Attacking the "soft bigotry of low expectations" became his battle cry, backed up by forceful action.[1]

In subsequent years, I have continued to follow the Nation's Report Card reports from the sidelines. For reasons that will be debated forever, academic progress in the nation's schools after the Bush years lost momentum and stalled. Then came the pandemic, and in its aftermath NAEP performance sank to unprecedented low levels. Specifically, fourth-grade mathematics scores jumped from 226 in 2000 to 240 in 2009, leveled off at 240 through 2017, rose just one point to 241 in 2019, and then dropped to 236 in 2022. At the eighth-grade level in mathematics, scores increased from 273 in 2000 to 283 in 2009, stalled at 283 through 2017, dipped to 282 in 2019, and plunged to 274 in 2022. In the reading assessments, at grade 4, scores increased from 213 in 2000 to 221 in 2009, rose to 222 by 2017, dropped to 220 in 2019, and fell to 217 in 2022 At grade 8 in reading, scores climbed from 263 in 1998 to 264 in 2009, jumped to 267 in 2017, slipped to 263 in 2019, and dropped to 260 in 2022.[2]

Given the size of the samples in the NAEP assessment process, a one-point change up or down is typically statistically significant. That reality underscores the importance of the trendline with mathematics and reading at both the fourth- and eighth-grade levels since 2000. The takeaway is the clear evidence that improvements occurred in the first decade of the current century, flattened out in the

---

1. "U.S. Students Show Progress in Math and Reading, Minority Students Post Some of the Larger Gains," National Assessment Governing Board, 2007 Nation's Report Card, September 25, 2007, www.nagb.gov/naep -subject-areas/multi-subject-archive/reading-and-mathematics/2007.
2. "Largest Score Declines in NAEP Mathematics at Grades 4 and 8 Since Initial Assessments in 1990" and "Scores Decline in NAEP Reading at Grades 4 and 8 Compared to 2019," Reports, www.nationsreportcard.gov.

second decade, and plunged to the lowest levels in NAEP history in the early years of the third decade.

The pandemic obviously had an impact on student performance in the 2022 assessment. However, performance stagnation had lingered for most of the second decade of this century. The national *Education Week* noted in a byline article by Sarah Sparks that the pandemic "provided more of a tipping point than a single push. Math scores have been falling off for years." In that same article, Sparks quoted US Secretary of Education Miguel Cardona as saying "let's be very clear here: The data prior to the pandemic did not reflect an education system that was on the right track. The pandemic simply made it worse. It took poor performance and dropped it down even further. As an educator and as a parent, that's heartbreaking and it's horrible. It's an urgent call to action."[3]

While no clear-cut answer as to why scores in both mathematics and reading stalled after 2009 is apparent, I can see some clues. For one, the Bush administration ended, and as typically happens with a change of leadership, the agenda changed. Gone from the arena were the strong voices of President Bush, Education Secretary Margaret Spellings, Darv Winick and scores of other administration leaders who created and nurtured the No Child Left Behind initiative. The death of Senator Ted Kennedy, a Democrat who was a staunch supporter of NCLB, only added to the vacuum in leadership support.

Concurrent with the change in presidential leadership, the National Governors Association and the Council of Chief State School Officers launched the Common Core initiative. From outside looking in, my view is that throughout all of the national debate about Common Core, the Nation's Report Card stayed above the fray. The National Assessment Governing Board held true to its

---

3. Sarah Sparks, "Explaining That Steep Drop in Math Scores on NAEP: 5 Takeaways," *Education Week*, October 24, 2022.

commitment to maintain the National Assessment of Educational Progress as the gold standard in education assessment. However, the Common Core debate diminished the visibility of NAEP, and the momentum created by NAEP assessment results in the Bush years stalled. Is that why student performance as measured by the Nation's Report Card stagnated after the Bush years? There is no clear answer to that question. Historians of the future will have a field day addressing the reasons why. At the same time, the evidence is clear that the Nation's Report Card in the first decade of this century was a prime example of a government initiative that worked while everything going on around it was floundering or failing.

Sadly, my wife Shawna Lea died in early 2013 after a six-month battle with pancreatic cancer. In October of 2016, I married Barbara Cappiello. Ironically, Barbara and I were enjoying a stay on the same Florida beach where my Nation's Report Card story had begun two decades before, when I once again spoke with Darv Winick about the National Assessment Governing Board. It had been more than ten years since Winick and I had left the stage of leadership, but I had shared electronically with him an early draft of this book. He responded with substantive feedback, followed by a phone call with me a few days later.

Here we were, two former strangers who were now trusted friends, one nearly ninety years old and the other just turning eighty, looking back to memories of a time we both cherished. As Winick talked about my draft in both the electronic feedback and subsequent phone call, he sprinkled his feedback with words and phrases like legacy, earning respect, building trust, and focusing on effective communication. Noting that our experience base was firmly built on more than thirty years of extensive leadership roles in education, media, and public service, he labeled our combined service in the public sector as a game changer for the Nation's Report Card team. We shared the belief that being experienced outsiders operating inside the Beltway had been a clear asset.

"I credit you with a great improvement in reporting and report preparation," Winick said. "You understood my desire to speak directly to the public. This may be a most important legacy of our time."

Clearly enjoying the "memory jog" from reading my manuscript, Winick shared his memories. Some I knew, others I did not. My favorite was his story about how we had been perceived at that time. "Not only were we independent," Winick said, "but according to talk within the education sector, we had immediate access to the president. Even after our retirements, I was introduced as someone who could phone the president. Fortunately, I never had to test this implied access, although once when NCES rejected our plans to expand high school testing because of cost, I suggested that I would check with the president. Within twenty-four hours, IES (Institute of Education Sciences) found sufficient funds."

As Winick had done from day one of our working relationship, he focused on the importance of press relations. He always had a way with words spoken softly but firmly. "Public relations activities were dramatically changed on our watch," he said. "We moved information flow from research and interest-group communities to the public in a big way. You were out front in this effort. I believe that you were present when representatives of the research contractors and the DC press corps met with us, saying it was impossible for us to have meetings around the country. They were not budgeted for travel, they said. Our response was, 'We will miss you.' They never missed a meeting, regardless of location."

Winick also recalled, with some humor, the early questions about my Democratic background and his tie to the Bush administration. "Once when asked if the board was sufficiently bipartisan, I said, 'No. We are nonpartisan.' I believe that it was important that we were seen as above specific party or interest group. I think that you and the staff performed well in this regard. You note correctly that the board was seen as independent and had excellent relationships with congressional members and their staff. I was personally informed by both Senators Kennedy and Alexander to call if we received any undue pressure."

Winick's incisive summation brought closure to what had been, for me, a magical story of a government initiative that had worked and made a difference. The first decade of the new century was a heady time for the Nation's Report Card team. We succeeded by building trust, earning respect, and communicating effectively. Taking NAEP from the backrooms to Main Street will always be a point of pride, I believe, for all of us who were involved.

For two former strangers from Texas and Tennessee, who bonded closely for six years, this brief shining moment of reminiscing reflected career high points. We parted knowing that we had played a major role in changing forever the way educators, the media, and the general public interpret and use student assessment results.

www.ingramcontent.com/pod-product-compliance
Lightning Source LLC
LaVergne TN
LVHW092327221025
824101LV00035B/971